A REBEL'S
RECOLLECTIONS

GEORGE CARY EGGLESTON

————— ◆●▶ —————

INTRODUCTION BY GAINES M. FOSTER

LOUISIANA STATE UNIVERSITY PRESS

BATON ROUGE AND LONDON

Introduction copyright © 1996 by Louisiana State University Press
LSU Press edition offset from 1959 Indiana University Press edition by
    arrangement with Indiana University Press
Manufactured in the United States of America

Louisiana Paperback Edition, 1996

05 04 03 02 01 00 99 98 97 96   5 4 3 2 1

LIBRARY OF CONGRESS CATALOGING-IN-PUBLICATION DATA

Eggleston, George Cary, 1839–1911.
    A rebel's recollections / George Cary Eggleston ; introduction by
    Gaines M. Foster. – Louisiana paperback ed.
        p.   cm.
    ISBN 0-8071-2125-8 (p : alk. paper)
    1. United States–History–Civil War, 1861–1865–Personal
narratives, Confederate.   2. Eggleston, George Cary, 1839–1911.
    3. Confederate States of America–History.   I. Title.
    E487.E32   1996
    973.7'82–dc20   96-27324
    [B]   CIP

The paper in this book meets the guidelines for permanence and durability of
the Committee on Production Guidelines for Book Longevity of the Council
on Library Resources. ∞

DEDICATION

I wish to dedicate this book to my brother, Edward Eggleston; and even if there were no motives of affection impelling me thereto, I should still feel bound to inscribe his name upon this page, as an act of justice, in order that those critics who confounded me with him, when I put forth a little novel a year ago, may have no chance to hold him responsible for my political as they did for my literary sins.

CONTENTS

———◄•►———

INTRODUCTION

A FTER reading *A Rebel's Recollections,* William Dean Howells observed, one "thoroughly likes the author." Howells found Eggleston's reminiscences of the American Civil War entertaining; others have called them charming. *A Rebel's Recollections* is indeed both, in part because of Eggleston's prose. A confessed "extemporaneous" writer, Eggleston claimed that he never knew when he wrote "a first sentence or a first chapter what the second was to be" and denied that he ever revised. In fact, there is little overall narrative structure to *A Rebel's Recollections.* Instead, it offers a series of rambling chapters on different aspects of the war. This "extemporaneous" quality gives the book an immediacy enlivened by a subtle humor and vivid, illustrative anecdotes. Eggleston, who never forgot the horrors of war, preferred to write about "the delights of the war game" and how it called forth "some of the noblest qualities of human nature" and bred "chivalric sentiments."[1] This delight in soldiering and chivalry gives Eggleston's book a romantic air traditionally associated with memoirs of the Lost Cause. Neither the casualness of the narrative nor the fond memories of the war, however, obscure Eggleston's insight into the problems of the Confederacy. On certain topics, Jefferson Davis most prominent among them, Eggleston could be sternly critical. After finishing *A Rebel's Recollections,* Davis probably thoroughly *dis*liked its author.

George Cary Eggleston was born not in the South but in Vevay, Indiana, on November 26, 1839. Nevertheless, he took great pride in having descended on both sides of his family from distinguished southern, and more particularly Virginian, stock. The Egglestons first came to Virginia in 1635, and during the American Revolution George's grandfather served as second-in-command to General "Lighthorse" Harry Lee. Joseph Cary Eggleston, George's father, grew up in Virginia, graduated from the College of William and Mary, but then renounced his inheritance and moved to Indiana. He did so in part to make his fortune in the expanding West, but also because of his reservations about slavery. In Indiana, Joseph married Mary Jane Craig, whose family had come from Kentucky after freeing its slaves. Before Kentucky, her family, too, had been Virginians.[2]

Despite his doubts about slavery, the expatriate Joseph regaled his children with stories of his home state and imbued his sons with an appreciation for Virginia's values, especially concepts of honor. George, though only seven when his father died, apparently learned these lessons well. Even as a youth, he displayed a fierce independence, pride, and concern for appearances, all tempered by a respect for honesty, personal responsibility, and loyalty. George's father and, perhaps even more, his mother emphasized education. Their home was filled with books, and all the Eggleston children attended school. As adults, all four would try their hands at writing, and the oldest, Edward Eggleston, would produce the popular *Hoosier Schoolmaster*. Far better known than George, Edward was an early literary realist as well as, later in life, a pioneer in social and cultural history.

Descended from Virginians, the Eggleston children grew up in the midst of stern, midwestern Methodism. Two years after George was born, his parents converted to that faith during a revival. Edward, too, took to it, but George later claimed to be born "a skeptic, a doubter, an inquirer" and clearly chafed under the piety of his family and neighbors.[3] When George was seven, his father died. Four years later his mother remarried, this time to a Methodist minister, but George never got along well with his stepfather or stepsiblings. The new family moved four times, on each occasion to a different town in Indiana, at last returning to Vevay when his stepfather took a job with the American Bible Society that required him to travel. Not long thereafter, George enrolled in Indiana Asbury (now DePauw) University, from which, during his second year, he and other students were sent home for refusing to accept the faculty's punishment. When the board overruled the faculty, most students returned, but on a point of honor George refused to do so. He taught school and, for a brief period, clerked in a store. Then, in 1857, George's mother died, and George left Indiana to live with his uncle in his father's former home in Amelia County, Virginia.

The eighteen-year-old did not simply move to Virginia, he embraced it. He adopted many of its values, within four years would go to war in its behalf, and would build his postwar literary career primarily on celebrating its prewar civilization. This embrace, immediate and total, is curious given his parents' views on slavery and, especially, his brother's experience. Edward had moved to Virginia two years before George but, appalled by its lack of religious fervor and disgusted by slavery, soon returned to Indiana. George, on the other hand, found Virginia, as he put it much later, "the complete realization of romance, the actual embodiment of poetry, a dream life of exquisite perfection."[4] Why did this midwestern youth become so enthusiastic a Virginian, indeed literally a professional Virginian?

Eggleston explained it by citing his prior love of poetry and romantic history as well as his sense of relief at escaping the commercialism of an expanding West. He also claimed that he found Virginians' culture of honor a means to preserve proper behavior without a reliance on God to justify it. These rationales, offered long after the fact, hardly seem convincing explanations for the behavior of an eighteen-year-old, even a born skeptic who had clerked in a store. They do, though, help explain why antebellum Virginia continued to be an important and useful mythic image for Eggleston long after he had left it. His reasons for initially falling in love with plantation society in Virginia may have had more personal origins. Since he was eleven, George had lost his father, had not gotten along well with his stepfather or his new siblings, had moved several times, and finally, had lost his mother. An "orphan" and a wanderer, he arrived in Amelia County and was welcomed and embraced by his father's relatives.[5] He found there, perhaps, a sense of place and family he had not had since he was a small child. And, of course, it did not hurt that on his second day in Virginia an uncle promised to pay his way to college and law school.

Of course, his father's stories had prepared Eggleston to feel at home in Virginia. Edward had heard them, too. But unlike his older brother, George had never been comfortable in the strenuous, deeply religious environment of rural Methodism and found Amelia County an escape from it. George was also untroubled by slavery. "I think," he wrote Edward in 1858, "[slavery is] a good institution, or at least productive of more good than evil." He felt so in large measure because of his views on African Americans: "After eighteen months residence in the south I am thoroughly convinced that negroes are unfit to be free."[6] His views changed little after that; his paternalistic racism surfaces briefly in *A Rebel's Recollections* and more prominently in much of his later writing.

Having found a home in Virginia, George set out to create a life there. He went to Richmond College, studied law, and had begun to practice in 1861 when the war interrupted. Although he had opposed secession, on April 9, 1861, Eggleston enlisted in the Confederate army. He joined the First Regiment of Virginia Cavalry, serving initially under J. E. B. Stuart and, later, Fitzhugh Lee, who once rescued Eggleston when he had a horse shot out from under him. In 1862, worrying about his younger brother serving there and suspecting that the fighting was going to shift to the south, Eggleston requested and received a transfer to the South Carolina coast. There he joined an artillery unit, but his expectations went unrealized. He saw action only during the Battle of Pocotaligo. His unit, the Nelson (Virginia) Light Artillery, returned to Virginia in 1863. With no horses and assigned to no battalion, it served as provost guards. During this period, then

Sergeant-Major Eggleston spent his time defending soldiers before courts-martial. The following year, his unit requested rifles with which to become a battalion of sharpshooters and as such fought at the Wilderness. At Petersburg, Eggleston took command of a mortar fort. During these last two years of the war he saw considerable action, suffered at least one wound, and at the end surrendered with Lee at Appomattox.

The surrender devastated Eggleston, as it did many Confederates. Not a few of them fled north or west; Eggleston did both. Abandoning Virginia, physically at least, Eggleston first went "home" to Indiana. Next he moved to Cairo, Illinois, where he worked as a counsel in a large mercantile firm and, in 1868, married Marion Craggs. He did not like the work; he relocated to Memphis, then to Mississippi, where he practiced law, which he liked even less. So in 1870, with, as he put it, "a wife, one child, a little household furniture, and no money at all," Eggleston took up residence in New York City.[7] He secured a job as a reporter on the Brooklyn *Union* and then became managing editor of the weekly magazine *Hearth and Home*, hired by his brother, who had just become its editor. Edward, too sickly for the army, had lived in the Midwest during the war, tried preaching but, by the time he moved to New York, had given it up (save for one brief period serving a Brooklyn pulpit) to be a journalist and writer.

Through Edward's connections and his own as managing editor, Eggleston began to make friends among northern writers. In 1874 one of them, William Dean Howells, editor of the *Atlantic Monthly*, asked George to write a series of articles on his wartime experiences. Both Howells and his magazine were known for their antisouthern views. Howells had hated slavery and continued to criticize southern civilization into the late 1860s. But in the early seventies he became disillusioned with Reconstruction. That, along with friends such as Eggleston, helped moderate, though never transformed, his views about southerners and made him willing to publish southern writers. There may have been other considerations behind his request, as well. A rival magazine, *Lippincott's*, had prospered soliciting southern authors and subscribers, and just the year before another competitor, *Scribner's Monthly*, drew wide notice with the publication of Edward King's "The Great South" series, which celebrated changes in the region.[8] After some deliberation, recounted in the original preface, Eggleston agreed to undertake the project Howells suggested. The first article, in this edition the second chapter, appeared in the *Atlantic* in June, 1874, with others following one each month for six months. Even before the first appeared, the publishers Hurd & Houghton agreed to bring the articles out in book form under the title Eggleston had used for the magazine series, with the addition of two new chapters, the present Chapters 7 and 8. As the preface to the 1905 edition explains, what is now the first chapter was written at about the same time as the other articles and appeared in the *Atlantic* in November, 1875, but it was added to the book only with that edition.

He agreed to write the book, Eggleston told his old friend Virginia author John Esten Cooke in 1874, "principally to amuse & interest my readers" but also because it provided a good opportunity "for running in bits of fact which may change some people's views of the South & Southerners, for both are sadly misunderstood."[9] As a result, *A Rebel's Recollections* can be read, and should be read, in two ways, as one soldier's entertaining and insightful memories of the Civil War and as a postwar southern plea for northern respect.

For a war memoir, *A Rebel's Recollections* contains surprisingly few descriptions of military conflicts; a reader seeking blood will find little, and even guts are celebrated more in the abstract than in action. What descriptions there are of military engagements can, for the most part, be trusted. The historian David Donald checked Eggleston's account against the official record and found it dependable, though occasionally exaggerated or dramatized. In particular, Donald questioned the description of Lee at Appomattox—both the story of surrendering his sword and the report that he seemed to be in agony.[10] Eggleston's contributions, however, rarely involve questions of fact about major historical events. They concern matters of perception. While Eggleston's observations should, of course, be weighed against those of others, his memoir yields many important insights about the Confederacy.

The best parts of *A Rebel's Recollections* are, perhaps, its compelling portraits of individuals. Eggleston was a careful observer with a gift for characterization. The fullest and best is of J. E. B. Stuart. Eggleston served for a time as Stuart's clerk, which gave him close access to the general. The portrait also benefits from Stuart's personification of the culture of honor that Eggleston believed in and celebrated in his writing. The sketches of Robert E. Lee and Stonewall Jackson, though not as long, are still good, with that of Jackson the better of the two. Eggleston also provides some realistic portraits of enlisted soldiers with whom he served.

In addition to its sketches of individuals, *A Rebel's Recollections* offers important insights into life within the Confederacy. Eggleston makes obligatory reference to the unanimity of the southern people and generally paints them in heroic hues. Yet he also reveals internal problems and governmental incompetence within the South. His discussion of Confederate finance and the resulting rampant inflation, delivered with considerable humor, reveals how people adjusted to the scarcities the war brought and how speculators exploited the situation. In other places, Eggleston lampoons the use of military passes and the provost system. He condemns the army's commissary system, blaming its failures on Commissary General Lucius B. Northrop, kindly unnamed in the text but unkindly suggested to be insane. Most important, *A Rebel's Recollections* treats almost all Confederate politicians with condescension and levels its severest criticism at the most prominent of them all, President Jefferson Davis.

These sections of the book echo the scorn, heard in most wars, of frontline soldiers for those in the rear. And, of course, criticism of Davis was not uncommon among all kinds of southerners during and immediately after the war. Eggleston's contempt for Davis, though, seems especially vehement and may have been, in part, personal. The president's worst perfidy—mentioned three times—was unloading a train of supplies that should have gone to Lee at Appomattox in order to hasten his own escape from Richmond. Eggleston was with Lee. Eggleston's criticism of Davis and his other tales of Confederate incompetence may be exaggerated, but they are not without merit and remind readers that the Confederates faced challenges, if not enemies, within as well as without their lines.

The attacks on Davis and other politicians also contribute, perhaps unintentionally, to Eggleston's second stated purpose in the book—explaining the South to the North. In the years after Appomattox, many white southerners wanted some admission or sign that their former foes thought they had acted nobly and fought bravely. Indeed, few southerners would accept sectional reconciliation without such an acknowledgment. It had to do, in part, with the system of honor, southerners' need to seek societal approval as a ratification of their behavior. A northerner by birth and residence, but a former Confederate imbued if not obsessed with the ideal of honor, Eggleston proved a natural advocate of the South's case.[11]

Though added later, Chapter 1 serves as a logical beginning to Eggleston's appeal. Many northerners blamed secession and the war on what they considered the hotheaded, violent aristocrats of the South—the villainous, corrupt slavepower. Therefore, to create northern sympathy for the South, the slaveholders' image needed to be rehabilitated. Eggleston's sketch of life in antebellum Virginia tries to do just that. It concedes, indeed revels in, the fact that the slaveholders were aristocrats who exercised power. But these aristocrats were well informed on political issues and listened to one another. They were also, in Eggleston's account, reasonable, religious, industrious, intelligent, cultured—thoroughly attractive and not at all threatening.

Chapter 2, the first of the original articles, explicitly asks northern readers to become Confederates for a time, to see things as southerners had seen them. To help them do so, Eggleston does not present the strident constitutional defense of state sovereignty and the legal right of secession offered in memoirs by Alexander Stephens, Jefferson Davis, or some other former Confederates. Eggleston does present secession as a constitutional right, but also calls it a revolutionary act. He develops neither idea, however; rather he retells the story of Virginia's decision to secede in a way that renders ardent secessionists blowhards, if not cowards. Most Virginians, Eggleston suggests, were reluctant rebels forced to withdraw from the Union over a point of honor. The constitutional issue of state sovereignty becomes secondary, and slavery has nothing to do with it. Such an interpretation could be rendered plausible for Virginia, and Eggleston makes Virginia the South. He simply ignores the very different road to secession of South Carolina and the lower South. Eggleston's relative silence on slavery and other emotional issues that could still exacerbate sectional tensions persists throughout the book. His only reference to slaves or blacks comes in a brief celebration of their wartime loyalty. He generally has kind words for the behavior of the northern armies and ignores Reconstruction altogether. Among southerners, only white women, whose loyalty he praises, are said to continue to cherish intense hatred for the Yankees. But hostile southern women ripe for conversion by northern men would soon become stock characters in reconciliation fiction.[12]

Even the women, though, are discussed only briefly. Eggleston reserves most of his praise for the officers and soldiers in the field. To his credit, Eggleston makes clear that Confederate soldiers did not report for duty full-blown heroes; only after being trained and gaining combat experience did they become the successful—even heroic—fighters they were in the latter part of the war. By lauding this hard-earned heroism and evoking the hardships of the war, Eggleston makes it easier for northerners to be Confederates for a time. By omitting descriptions of battles, which might have reminded northerners of the war's cost, by scorning politicians, and by remaining silent on the war's explosive issues, Eggleston centers his former foes' attention on experiences with which they, especially the soldiers among them, could identify. Northern readers of *A Rebel's Recollections* are left with an image of Confederate soldiers who were patriotic, brave defenders of honor, fighting only for an "abstraction" and not out of any deep hatred for the Union, the North, or American political principles.

How important *A Rebel's Recollections* became in winning northern respect for southern fighters and, through that, fostering sectional reconciliation, is difficult to judge. The 1905 preface suggests that Eggleston's defense of the South generated considerable
controversy. By the time of the book's publication, however, hostility had dissipated. Eggleston told of being feted by other New
York writers and reported favorable reviews in New England
newspapers. Eggleston's friend and editor Howells judged that the
series "helped our readers to understand that those opposed to the
Union in the late war were as sincere as its friends, and were moved
by a patriotism which differed from ours only in being mistaken."
Three years later, a second edition appeared, proving, the literary
editor of *Harper's* reported with a sneer, that "its merits as a modest contribution to history from the Southern stand-point have
had kindly recognition."[13] Certainly the emphasis on sincere if
mistaken patriotism and honorable martial glory became the basis
for much of the sectional reconciliation that followed over the
next three decades. *A Rebel's Recollections* played a role in that, but
probably no more than several other books or articles.

The influence of *A Rebel's Recollections* on southern views was
perhaps less significant. Some of its themes did become staples of
the Lost Cause: the celebration of Lee, Jackson, and Stuart; the
portrait of loyal southern women; the account of the faithful slave.
But by the 1890s, conservative white southerners did not enjoy
talk about exercising a right of revolution, and many even re-
sented the use of the term *rebel*. More important, Davis' reputation had been rehabilitated, and few southerners wrote so honestly about failings within the Confederate army and government.
Neither the United Confederate Veterans nor the United Daughters of the Confederacy placed *A Rebel's Recollections* on its list of
approved books.[14]

Eggleston probably did not worry much about this as he prepared his introduction for a fourth edition in 1905. He took satisfaction in the fact that the book had contributed to sectional
reconciliation and, ever modest in print, that it "enjoyed a degree
of public favor that is perhaps beyond its merits." One review of

the new edition observed that *A Rebel's Recollections* "still outranks in interest almost all other reminiscences of the Civil War."[15] Twentieth-century historians have continued to cite it, and the appearance of this edition, the seventh, surely says something.

After publication of his *Recollections,* Eggleston continued to live in New York City, yet another southerner who celebrated the South while living elsewhere. Eggleston always maintained that the Virginia he loved and championed existed only in the past. The war had changed it; he could never go home again. In New York he worked at several newspapers and publishing jobs, including stints as a literary editor for William Cullen Bryant's New York *Evening Post* and as an editorial writer for Joseph Pulitzer's *World.* He continued to publish books and always planned to quit the newspaper business to devote himself full-time to this. Finally, in 1900, he did—and wrote another twenty books, bringing his total output to over thirty. They included how-to books, stories for boys, historical novels, and histories. Several of the novels were set in antebellum or Civil War Virginia. He also returned to the war in two of his histories: an interesting collection of fact and fiction titled *Southern Soldier Stories* (1898) and the able, relatively objective *The History of the Confederate War* (1910). By no means did Eggleston ever become a major writer; *A Rebel's Recollections* is undoubtedly his best-known, and best, book.

After his retirement from journalism, Eggleston remained active in New York literary circles. He spent his winters in the city and his summers upstate, on beautiful Lake George. There, in 1911, Eggleston died, according to one obituary, after a "long and sorrowful" illness that "he bore heroically."[16] A Virginia gentleman, ever mindful of his honor, would have liked to have read that.

GAINES M. FOSTER

NOTES

1.   William Dean Howells, "Recent Literature," *Atlantic Monthly,* XXXV (February, 1875), 238; David Donald, "Introduction" to A Rebel's Recollections (Bloomington, 1959), 9. Eggleston quotations from George Cary Eggleston, *Recollections of a Varied Life* (New York, 1910), 81, 339–40.

2.   The account of Eggleston's life that follows is based primarily on Eggleston, *Recollections;* Eggleston, *The First of the Hoosiers: Reminiscences of Edward Eggleston* (Philadelphia, 1903); John Calvin Metcalf, "George Cary Eggleston," in *The Library of Southern Literature,* ed. Edwin A. Alderman and Joel Chandler Harris (17 vols.; Atlanta, 1909–1923), XV, 1525–32; Louise E. Callison, "George Cary Eggleston: A Biographical and Critical Study" (Ph.D. dissertation, Case Western Reserve University, 1969); and William Randel, *Edward Eggleston* (New York, 1963). On southern honor see Bertram Wyatt-Brown, *Southern Honor: Ethics & Behavior in the Old South* (New York, 1982).

3.   Quotation from Eggleston, *First of the Hoosiers,* 223.

4.   *Ibid.,* 213.

5.   George Cary Eggleston to Mary M. Hayne, May 10, 1889, Paul H. Hayne Papers, Manuscripts Department, Perkins Library, Duke University.

6.   George Eggleston to Edward Eggleston, October 26, 1858, quoted in Randel, *Eggleston,* 48–49.

7.   Eggleston, *Recollections,* 99.

8.   Daniel Aaron, *The Unwritten War: American Writers and the Civil War* (New York, 1973), 121–32; Rayburn S. Moore, "Southern Writers and Northern Literary Magazines, 1865–1890" (Ph.D. dissertation, Duke University, 1956). On Eggleston and other southerners going North, see Daniel E. Sutherland, *The Confederate Carpetbaggers* (Baton Rouge, 1988).

9.   George Cary Eggleston to John Esten Cooke, April 26, 1874, John Esten Cooke Papers, Manuscripts Department, Perkins Library, Duke University.

10.   Donald, "Introduction," 13.

11.   These and following comments on reconciliation and the South's view of history rely on Gaines M. Foster, *Ghosts of the Confederacy: Defeat, the Lost Cause, and the Emergence of the New South, 1865–1913* (New York, 1987).

12.   See Nina Silber, *The Romance of Reunion: Northerners and the South, 1865–1900* (Chapel Hill, 1993).

13.   Howells, "Recent Literature," 238; "Editor's Literary Review," *Harper's New Monthly Magazine,* LVIII (December, 1878), 150.

14.   *Sixth Annual Meeting and Reunion of the United Confederate Veterans* (1896), 46–48; *Minutes of the Eleventh Annual Convention of the United Daughters of the Confederacy* (1904), 201–203.

15.   *Outlook,* April 29, 1905, p. 134, quoted in Callison, "Eggleston," 34.

16.   "In Memoriam," *Bookman,* XXXV (May, 1912), 326.

PREFACE TO THE
FIRST EDITION

———————•——

LUNCHING one day with Oliver Johnson, the best "original abolitionist" I ever knew, I submitted to him the question I was debating with myself, namely, whether I might write this little volume of reminiscences without fear of offending excellent people, or, still worse, reanimating prejudices that happily were dying. His reply was, "Write, by all means. Prejudice is the first-born of ignorance, and it never outlives its father. The only thing necessary now to the final burial of the animosity existing between the sections is that the North and the South shall learn to know and understand each other. Anything which contributes to this hastens the day of peace and harmony and brotherly love which every good man longs for."

Upon this hint I have written, and if the reading of these pages shall serve, in never so small a degree, to strengthen the kindly feelings which have grown up of late between the foemen of ten years ago, I shall think my labor well expended.

I have written chiefly of the things I saw for myself, and yet this is in no sense the story of my personal adventures. I never wore a star on my collar, and every reader of mili-

tary novels knows that adventures worth writing about
never befall a soldier below the rank of major.

G. C. E.

October, 1874

PREFACE TO THE
FOURTH EDITION

———— ◆ ————

A REBEL'S RECOLLECTIONS was published in 1874. It has ever since enjoyed a degree of public favor that is perhaps beyond its merits.

However that may be, my friends among the historians and the critical students of history have persuaded me that, for the sake of historical completeness, I should include in this new edition of the book the prefatory essay on "The Old Régime in the Old Dominion," which first appeared in the *Atlantic Monthly* for November, 1875.

I am doing so with the generous permission of Messrs. Houghton, Mifflin, & Co., publishers of the *Atlantic Monthly*.

The scholars have said to me and to my publishers that during its thirty years of life the book has become a part of that body of literature to which historians must look as the sources of history. They have urged that the introductory chapter, now for the first time included in the volume, is an essential part of that material of history.

The story of the book and of this introductory chapter may, perhaps, have some interest for the reader. In that belief I tell it here.

In the year, 1873, I was editing the weekly periodical,

Hearth and Home. I went to Boston to secure certain contributions of literary matter. There, for the first time, I met Mr. William Dean Howells, then editor of the *Atlantic Monthly*—now recognized as the foremost creative and critical writer of America.

In the course of our conversation, Mr. Howells asked me why I should not write my reminiscences of life as a Southern soldier. At that time war passions had only just begun to cool, and so I answered that it would be hardly fair to the publishers of *Hearth and Home* for me in that way to thrust upon the readers of that periodical the fact that its editor had been a Rebel soldier.

"Oh, I didn't mean," answered Mr. Howells, "that you should write your reminiscences for *Hearth and Home.* I want you to write them for the *Atlantic.*"

I put the matter aside for a time. I wanted to think of it, and I wanted to consult my friends concerning the propriety of doing what Mr. Howells had suggested. Then it was that I talked with Oliver Johnson, and received from him the advice reported in the preface to the first edition of this book, which is printed on another page.

An arrangement was at once made with Mr. Howells that I should write seven of the nine papers composing the book, for publication in the *Atlantic,* the two other papers being reserved in order to "give freshness" to the volume when it should appear.

After the first paper was published, Mr. Howells wrote me that it had brought a hornets' nest about his ears, but that he was determined to go on with the series.

After the second paper appeared, he wrote me a delightful letter, saying that the hornets had "begun to sing psalms in his ears," in view of the spirit and temper of my work.

After all the papers were published, and on the day on

which the book, with its two additional chapters, appeared, there was held at the Parker House in Boston a banquet in celebration of the fifteenth anniversary of the founding of the *Atlantic*. At that dinner, and without warning, I was toasted as the author of the latest book of Civil War reminiscences. I made a feeble little speech in reply, but I found that the spirit in which I had written *A Rebel's Recollections* had met with cordial response from the New England audience. A company of "original abolitionists" had even planned to give me a dinner, all my own, with nobody present but original abolitionists and my Rebel self.

In the same way the book was received by the press, especially in New England, until I was satisfied that my work had really ministered somewhat to that reconciliation between North and South which I had hoped to help forward.

Some months later, in 1875, I wrote the article on the old Virginian life, and sent it to Mr. Howells. Mindful of his editorial injunction to confine articles to six magazine pages in length, I condensed what I had to say into that space. Then for the first time in my life I had an experience which has never since been repeated. Mr. Howells sent the article back to me with a request that I should *double its length*.

Some years later, the Authors Club gave a reception to Mr. Howells as our foremost living novelist, and it fell to me, as the presiding officer of the club's Executive Council, to escort the guest of the evening to the club. The war papers of the *Century Magazine* were at that time attracting a country-wide attention. As we drove to the club, Mr. Howells said to me:

"It was you and I who first conceived the idea of 'War Papers' as a magazine's chief feature. We were a trifle ahead of our time, I suppose, but our thought was the same as that which has since achieved so great a success."

In view of all these things, I inscribe this new and expanded edition of *A Rebel's Recollections* to the true godfather of the book—to

WILLIAM DEAN HOWELLS,

with admiration for his genius, with a grateful recollection of his helpfulness, and with personal affection.

GEORGE CARY EGGLESTON

The Authors Club
January, 1905

A REBEL'S RECOLLECTIONS

CHAPTER 1

THE OLD RÉGIME IN THE OLD DOMINION

———— ◆►► ————

IT WAS a very beautiful and enjoyable life that the Virginians led in that ancient time, for it certainly seems ages ago, before the war came to turn ideas upside down and convert the picturesque commonwealth into a commonplace, modern state. It was a soft, dreamy, deliciously quiet life, a life of repose, an old life, with all its sharp corners and rough surfaces long ago worn round and smooth. Everything fitted everything else, and every point in it was so well settled as to leave no work of improvement for anybody to do. The Virginians were satisfied with things as they were, and if there were reformers born among them, they went elsewhere to work changes. Society in the Old Dominion was like a well-rolled and closely packed gravel walk, in which each pebble has found precisely the place it fits best. There was no giving way under one's feet, no uncomfortable grinding of loose materials as one walked about over the firm and long-used ways of the Virginian social life.

Let me hasten to say that I do not altogether approve of that life by any means. That would be flat blasphemy against the god Progress, and I have no stomach for martyrdom, even of our modern, fireless sort. I frankly admit in the outset, therefore, that the Virginians of that old time, between which and the present there is so great a gulf fixed, were idle people. I am aware that they were, when I lived among them, extravagant for the most part, and in debt altogether. It were useless to deny that they habitually violated all the wise precepts laid down in the published writings of Poor Richard, and set at naught the whole gospel of thrift. But their way of living was nevertheless a very agreeable one to share or to contemplate, the more because there was nothing else like it anywhere in the land.

A whole community, with as nearly as possible nothing to do, is apt to develop a considerable genius for enjoyment, and the Virginians, during somewhat more than two centuries of earnest and united effort in that direction, had partly discovered and partly created both a science and an art of pleasant living. Add to idleness and freedom from business cares a climate so perfect that existence itself is a luxury within their borders, and we shall find no room for wonder that these people learned how to enjoy themselves. What they learned, in this regard, they remembered too. Habits and customs once found good were retained, I will not say carefully—for that would imply effort, and the Virginians avoided effort always—but tenaciously. The Virginians were born conservatives, constitutionally opposed to change. They loved the old because it was old, and disliked the new, if for no better reason, because it was new; for newness and rawness were well-nigh the same in their eyes.

This constitutional conservatism, without which their mode of life could never have been what it was, was nourished by both habit and circumstance. The Virginians were not much given to traveling beyond their own borders, and when they did go into the outer world it was only to find a manifestation of barbarism in every departure from their own prescriptive standards and models. Not that they were more bigoted than other people, for in truth I think they were not, but their bigotry took a different direction. They thought well of the old and the moss-grown, just as some people admire all that is new and garish and fashionable.

But chief among the causes of that conservatism which gave tone and color to the life we are considering was the fact that ancient estates were carefully kept in ancient families, generation after generation. If a Virginian lived in a particular mansion, it was strong presumptive proof that his father, his grandfather, and his great-grandfather had lived there before him. There was no law of primogeniture to be sure by which this was brought about, but there were well-established customs which amounted to the same thing. Family pride was a ruling passion, and not many Virginians of the better class hesitated to secure the maintenance of their family place in the ranks of the untitled peerage by the sacrifice of their own personal prosperity, if that were necessary, as it sometimes was. To the first-born son went the estate usually, by the will of the father and with the hearty concurrence of the younger sons, when there happened to be any such. The eldest brother succeeded the father as the head of the house, and took upon himself the father's duties and the father's burdens. Upon him fell the management of the estate; the maintenance of the mansion, which, under the laws of hospitality obtaining there, was no light task; the education of the younger sons and daughters; and last, though commonly not by any means least, the management of the hereditary debt. The younger children always had a home in the old mansion, secured to them by the will of their father sometimes, but secure enough in any case by a custom more binding than any law; and there were various other ways of providing for them.

If the testator were rich, he divided among them his bonds, stocks, and other personal property not necessary to the prosperity of the estate, or charged the head of the house with the payment of certain legacies to each. The mother's property, if she had brought a dower with her, was usually portioned out among them, and the law, medicine, army, navy, and church offered them genteel employment if they chose to set up for themselves. But these arrangements were subsidiary to the main purpose of keeping the estate in the family, and maintaining the mansion-house as a seat of elegant hospitality. So great was the importance attached to this last point, and so strictly was its observance enjoined upon the new lord of the soil, that he was frequently the least to be envied of all.

I remember a case in which a neighbor of my own, a very wealthy gentleman, whose house was always open and always full of guests, dying, left each of his children a plantation. To the eldest son, however, he gave the home estate, worth three or four times as much as any of the other plantations, and with it he gave the young man also a large sum of money. But he charged him with the duty of keeping open house there, at all times, and directed that the household affairs should be conducted always precisely as they had been during his own lifetime. The charge well-nigh outweighed the inheritance. The new master of the place lived in Richmond, where he was engaged in manufacturing, and after the death of the father the old house stood tenantless, but open as before. Its troops of softly shod servants swept and dusted and polished as of old. Breakfast, dinner, and supper were laid out every day at the accustomed hours, under the old butler's supervision, and as the viands grew cold his silent subordinates waited, trays in hand, at the back of the empty chairs during the full time appointed for each meal. I have stopped there for dinner, tea, or to spend

the night many a time, in company with one of the younger
sons who lived elsewhere, or with some relative of the family, or alone, as the case might be, and I have sometimes met
others there. But our coming or not was a matter of in-
difference. Guests knew themselves always welcome, but
whether guests came or not the household affairs suffered
no change. The destruction of the house by fire finally lifted
this burden from its master's shoulders, as the will did not
require him to rebuild. But while it stood, its master's large
inheritance was of very small worth to him. And in many
other cases the preference given to the eldest son in the distribution of property was in reality only a selection of his
shoulders to bear the family's burdens.

In these and other ways, old estates of greater or less
extent were kept together, and old families remained lords
of the soil. It is not easy to overestimate the effect of this
upon the people. A man to whom a great estate, with an
historic house upon it and an old family name attached to
it, has descended through several generations, could hardly
be other than a conservative in feeling and influence. These
people were the inheritors of the old and the established.
Upon them had devolved the sacred duty of maintaining
the reputation of a family name. They were no longer mere
individuals, whose acts affected only themselves, but were
chiefs and representatives of honorable houses, and as such
bound to maintain a reputation of vastly more worth than
their own. Their fathers before them were their exemplars,
and in a close adherence to family customs and traditions
lay their safety from unseemly lapses. The old furniture,
the old wainscot on the walls, the old pictures, the old house
itself, perpetually warned them against change as in itself
unbecoming and dangerous to the dignity of their race.

And so changes were unknown in their social system. As
their fathers lived, so lived they, and there was no feature

of their life pleasanter than its fixity. One always knew what to expect and what to do; there were no perplexing uncertainties to breed awkwardness and vexation. There was no room for shams and no temptation to vulgar display, and so shams and display had no chance to become fashionable.

Aside from the fact that the old and the substantial were the respectable, the social status of every person was so fixed and so well known that display was unnecessary on the part of the good families, and useless on the part of others. The old ladies constituted a college of heralds and could give you at a moment's notice any pedigree you might choose to ask for. The "goodness" of a good family was a fixed fact and needed no demonstration, and no *parvenu* could work his way into the charmed circle by vulgar ostentation or by any other means whatever. As one of the old dames used to phrase it, ostentatious people were thought to be "rich before they were ready."

As the good families gave law to the society of the land, so their chiefs ruled the State in a more positive and direct sense. The plantation owners, as a matter of course, constituted only a minority of the voting population, at least after the constitution of 1850 swept away the rule making the ownership of real estate a necessary qualification for suffrage; but they governed the State nevertheless as completely as if they had been in the majority. Families naturally followed the lead of their chiefs, voting together as a matter of clan pride, when no principle was involved, and so the plantation owners controlled directly a large part of the population. But a more important point was that the ballot was wholly unknown in Virginia until after the war, and as the large landowners were deservedly men of influence in the community, they had little difficulty, under a system of *viva-voce* voting, in carrying things their own way on all matters on which they were at all agreed among themselves. It often happened that a Whig would continue year after year to represent a Democratic district, or *vice versa,* in the Legislature or in Congress, merely by force of his large family connection and influence.

All this was an evil, if we choose to think it so. It was undemocratic certainly, but it worked wonderfully well, and the system was good in this at least, that it laid the foundations of politics among the wisest and best men the State had; for as a rule the planters were the educated men of the community, the reading men, the scholars, the thinkers, and well-nigh every one of them was familiar with the whole history of parties and of statesmanship. Politics was deemed a necessary part of every gentleman's education, and the youth of eighteen who could not recapitulate the doctrines set forth in the resolutions of 1798, or tell you the history of the Missouri Compromise or the Wilmot Proviso, was thought lamentably deficient in the very rudiments of culture. They had little to do, and they thought it the bounden duty of every free American citizen to prepare himself for the intelligent performance of his functions in the body politic. As a result, if Virginia did not always send wise men to the councils of the State and nation, she sent no politically ignorant ones at any rate.

It was a point of honor among Virginians never to shrink from any of the duties of a citizen. To serve as road-overseer or juryman was often disagreeable to men who loved ease and comfort as they did, but every Virginian felt himself in honor bound to serve whenever called upon, and that without pay, too, as it was deemed in the last degree disreputable to accept remuneration for doing the plain duty of a citizen.

It was the same with regard to the magistracy. Magistrates were appointed until 1850, and after that chosen by election, but under neither system was any man free to seek or to decline the office. Appointed or elected, one must serve, if he would not be thought to shirk his duties as a good man and citizen; and though the duties of the office were sometimes very onerous, there was practically no return of any sort made. Magistrates received no salary, and it was not customary for them to accept the small perquisites allowed them by law. Under the old constitution, the senior justice of each county was *ex-officio* high sheriff, and the farming of the shrievalty—for the high sheriff always farmed the office—yielded some pecuniary profit; but any one magistrate's chance of becoming the senior was too small to be reckoned in the account; and under the new constitution of 1850 even this was taken away, and the sheriffs were elected by the people. But to be a magistrate was deemed an honor, and very properly so, considering the nature of a Virginian magistrate's functions.

The magistrates were something more than justices of the peace. A bench of three or more of them constituted the County Court, a body having a wide civil and criminal jurisdiction of its own, and concurrent jurisdiction with the Circuit Court over a still larger field. This County Court sat monthly, and in addition to its judicial functions was charged with considerable legislative duties for the county, under a system which gave large recognition to the principle of local self-government. Four times a year it held grand-jury terms—an anomaly in magistrate's courts, I believe, but an excellent one as experience proved. In a large class of criminal cases a bench of five justices, sitting in regular term, was a court of oyer and terminer.

The concurrent jurisdiction of this County Court, as I have said, was very large, and as its sessions were monthly, while those of the circuit judges were held but twice a year, very many important civil suits involving considerable interests were brought there rather than before the higher tribunal. And here we encounter a very singular fact. The magistrates were usually planters, never lawyers, and yet, as the records show, the proportion of County-Court decisions reversed on appeal for error was always smaller than that of decisions made by the higher tribunals, in which regular judges sat. At the first glance this seems almost incredible, and yet it is a fact, and its cause is not far to seek. The magistrates, being unpaid functionaries, were chosen for their fitness only. Their election was a sort of choosing of arbitrators, and the men elected were precisely the kind of men commonly selected by honest disputants as umpires—men of integrity, probity, and intelligence. They came into court conscious of their own ignorance of legal technicalities, and disposed to decide questions upon principles of "right between man and man" rather than upon the letter of the law; and as the law is, in the main, founded upon precisely these principles of abstract justice, their decision usually proved sound in law as well as right in fact.

But the magistrates were not wholly without instruction even in technical matters of law. They learned a good deal by long service,—their experience often running over a period of thirty or forty years on the bench,—and, in addition to the skill which intelligent men must have gained in this way, they had still another resource. When the bench thought it necessary to inform itself on a legal point, the presiding magistrate asked in open court for the advice of counsel, and in such an event every lawyer not engaged in the case at bar, or in another involving a like principle, was under obligation to give a candid expression of his opinion.

The system was a very peculiar and interesting one, and in Virginia it was about the best also that could have been hit upon, though it is more than doubtful whether it would

work equally well anywhere else. All the conditions sur-
rounding it were necessary to its success, and those conditions were of a kind that cannot be produced at will; they
must grow. In the first place, the intelligence and culture
of a community must not be concentrated in certain centres, as is usually the case, especially in commercial and
manufacturing States, but must be distributed pretty evenly
over the country, else the material out of which such a
magistracy can be created will not be where it is needed;
and in the very nature of the case it cannot be imported
for the purpose. There must also be a public sentiment to
compel the best men to serve when chosen, and the best
men must be men of wealth and leisure, else they cannot
afford to serve, for such a magistracy must of necessity be
unpaid. In short, the system can work well only under the
conditions which gave it birth in Virginia, and those conditions will probably never again exist in any of these
States. It is a matter of small moment to the citizen of
Massachusetts or New York that Virginia once had a very
peculiar judiciary; but it is not a matter of light importance that our scheme of government leaves every State free
to devise for itself a system of local institutions adapted to
its needs and the character and situation of its people; that
it is not uniformity we have sought and secured in our
attempt to establish a government by the people, but a wise
diversity rather; that experience and not theory is our
guide; that our institutions are cut to fit our needs, and
not to match a fixed pattern; and that the necessities of
one part of the country do not prescribe a rule for another
part.

But this is not a philosophical treatise. Return we therefore to the region of small facts. It is a little curious that
with their reputed fondness for honorary titles of all kinds,
the Virginians never addressed a magistrate as "judge,"

even in that old time when the functions of the justice fairly entitled him to the name. And it is stranger still, perhaps, that in Virginia the members of the Legislature were never called "honorable," that distinction being held strictly in reserve for members of Congress and of the national cabinet. This fact seems all the more singular when we remember that in the view of Virginians the States were nations, while the general government was little more than their accredited agent, charged with the performance of certain duties and holding certain delegated powers which were subject to recall at any time.

I have said that every educated Virginian was acquainted with politics, but this is only half the truth. They knew the details quite as well as the general facts, and there were very many of them not politicians and never candidates for office of any kind who could give from memory an array of dates and other figures of which the *Tribune Almanac* would have no occasion to be ashamed. Not to know the details of the vote in Connecticut in any given year was to lay oneself open to a suspicion of incompetence; to confess forgetfulness of the "ayes and noes" on any important division in Congress was to rule oneself out of the debate as an ignoramus. I say debate advisedly, for there was always a debate on political matters when two Virginia gentlemen met anywhere except in church during sermon time. They argued earnestly, excitedly, sometimes even violently, but ordinarily without personal ill-feeling. In private houses they could not quarrel, being gentlemen and guests of a common host, or standing in the relation of guest and host to each other; in more public places—for they discussed politics in all places and at all times—they refrained from quarrelling because to quarrel would not have been proper. But they never lost an opportunity to

make political speeches to each other; alternately, sometimes, but quite as often both, or all, at once.

It would sometimes happen, of course, that two or more
gentlemen meeting would find themselves agreed in their
views, but the pleasure of indulging in a heated political
discussion was never foregone for any such paltry reason
as that. Finding no point on which they could disagree,
they would straightway join forces and do valiant battle
against the common enemy. That the enemy was not present
to answer made no difference. They knew all his positions
and all the arguments by which his views could be sustained
quite as well as he did, and they combated these. It was
funny, of course, but the participants in these one-sided
debates never seemed to see the ludicrous points of the
picture.

A story is told of one of the fiercest of these social political debaters—a story too well vouched for among his friends
to be doubted—which will serve, perhaps, to show how unnecessary the presence of an antagonist was to the successful
conduct of a debate. It was "at a dining-day," to speak in
the native idiom, and it so happened that all the guests
were Whigs, except Mr. E——, who was the staunchest of
Jeffersonian Democrats. The discussion began, of course,
as soon as the women left the table, and it speedily waxed
hot. Mr. E——, getting the ear of the company at the outset, laid on right and left with his customary vigor, rasping
the Whigs on their sorest points, arguing, asserting, de-
nouncing, demonstrating—to his own entire satisfaction—
for perhaps half an hour; silencing every attempt at inter-
ruption by saying:

"Now wait, please, till I get through; I'm one against
seven, and you must let me make my points. Then you can
reply."

He finished at last, leaving every Whig nerve quivering,

every Whig face burning with suppressed indignation, and every Whig breast full, almost to bursting, with a speech in reply. The strongest debater of them all managed to begin first, but just as he pronounced the opening words, Mr. E—— interrupted him.

"Pardon me," he said, "I know all your little arguments, so I'll go and talk with the girls for half an hour while you run them over; when you get through send for me, and I'll come and SWEEP YOU CLEAR OUT OF THE ARENA."

And with that the exasperating man bowed himself out of the dining-room.

But with all its ludicrousness, this universal habit of "talking politics" had its uses. In the first place, politics with these men was a matter of principle, and not at all a question of shrewd management. They knew what they had and what they wanted. Better still they knew every officeholder's record, and held each to a strict account of his stewardship.

Under the influence of this habit in social life, every man was constantly on his metal, of course, and every young man was bound to fortify himself for contests to come by a diligent study of history and politics. He must know as a necessary preparation for ordinary social converse all those things that are commonly left to the professional politicians. As well might he go into society in ignorance of yesterday's weather or last week's news, as without full knowledge of Benton's *Thirty Years' View,* and a familiar acquaintance with the papers in *The Federalist.* In short, this odd habit compelled thorough political education, and enforced upon every man old enough to vote an active, earnest participation in politics. Perhaps a country in which universal suffrage exists would be the better if both were more general than they are.

But politics did not furnish the only subjects of debate

among these people. They talked politics, it is true, whenever they met at all, but when they had mutually annihilated each other, when each had said all there was to say on the subject, they frequently turned to other themes. Of these, the ones most commonly and most vigorously discussed were points of doctrinal theology. The great battleground was baptism. Half the people were, perhaps, Baptists, and when Baptist and pedo-Baptist met they sniffed the battle at once,—that is to say, as soon as they had finished the inevitable discussion of politics.

On this question of Baptism each had been over the ground many hundreds of times, and each must have known when he put forth an argument what the answer would be. But this made no manner of difference. They were always ready to go over the matter again. I amused myself once by preparing a "part" debate on the subject. I arranged the remarks of each disputant in outline, providing each speech with its proper "cue," after the manner of stage copies of a play, and, taking a friend into my confidence, I used sometimes to follow the discussion, with my copy of it in hand, and, except in the case of a very poorly informed or wholly unpracticed debater, my "cues" and speeches were found to be amusingly accurate.

The Virginians were a very religious as well as a very polemical people, however, and I do not remember that I ever knew them, even in the heat of their fiercest discussions upon doctrine, to forget the brotherly kindness which lay as a broad foundation under their card-houses of creed. They believed with all their souls in the doctrines set down by their several denominations, and maintained them stoutly on all occasions; but they loved each other, attended each other's services, and joined hands right heartily in every good work.

There was one other peculiarity in their church relations worthy of notice. The Episcopal Church was once an establishment in Virginia, as every reader knows, but every reader does not know, perhaps, that even up to the outbreak of the war it remained in some sense an establishment in some parts of the State.

There were little old churches in many neighborhoods which had stood for a century or two, and the ancestors of the present generation had all belonged to them in their time. One of these churches I remember lovingly for its old traditions, for its picturesqueness, and for the warmth of the greeting its congregation gave me—not as a congregation but as individuals—when I, a lad half grown, returned to the land of my fathers. Every man and woman in that congregation had known my father and loved him, and nearly every one was my cousin, at least in the Virginian acceptation of that word. The church was Episcopal, of course, while the great majority, perhaps seven eighths of the people who attended it and supported it were members of other denominations—Baptists, Presbyterians, and Methodists. But they all felt themselves at home here. This was the old family church where their forefathers had worshiped, and under the shadow of which they were buried. They all belonged here no matter what other church might claim them as members. They paid the old clergyman's salary, served in the vestry, attended the services, kept church, organ, and church-yard in repair, and in all respects regarded themselves, and were held by others, as members here of right and by inheritance. It was church and family, instead of Church and State, and the sternest Baptist or Presbyterian among them would have thought himself wronged if left out of the count of this little church's membership. This was their heritage, their home, and the fact that they had also united themselves with churches of other denominations made no difference whatever in their feeling toward the old mother church, there in the woods, guarding and cherishing the dust of their dead.

All the people, young and old, went to church; it was both pleasant and proper to do so, though not all of them went for the sake of the sermon or the service. The churches were usually built in the midst of a grove of century oaks, and their surroundings were nearly always pleasantly picturesque. The gentlemen came on horseback, the ladies in their great lumbering, old-fashioned carriages, with an ebony driver in front and a more or less ebony footman or two behind. Beside the driver sat ordinarily the old "mammy" of the family, or some other equally respectable and respected African woman, whose crimson or scarlet turban and orange neckerchief gave a dash of color to the picture, a trifle barbaric, perhaps, in combination, but none the less pleasant in its effect for that. The young men came first, mounted on their superb riding horses, wearing great buckskin gauntlets and clad in full evening dress—that being *en règle* always in Virginia,—with the skirts of the coat drawn forward, over the thighs, and pinned in front, as a precaution against possible contact with the reeking sides of the hard-ridden steeds.

The young men came first to church, as I have said, and they did so for a purpose. The carriages were elegant and costly, many of them, but nearly all were extremely old-fashioned; perched high in air, they were not easy of entrance or exit by young women in full dress without assistance, and it was accounted the prescriptive privilege of the young men to render the needed service at the church door. When this preliminary duty was fully done, some of the youths took seats inside the church, but if the weather were fine many preferred to stroll through the woods, or to sit in little groups under the trees, awaiting the exit of the womankind, who must, of course, be chatted with and helped into their carriages again.

Invitations to dinner or to a more extended visit were in order the moment the service was over. Every gentleman went to dine with a friend, or took a number of friends to dine with him. But the arrangements depended largely upon the young women, who had a very pretty habit of visiting each other and staying a week or more, and these visits nearly always originated at church. Each young woman invited all the rest to go home with her, and after a deal of confused consultation, out of whose chaos only the feminine mind could possibly have extracted anything like a conclusion, two or three would win all the others to themselves, each taking half a dozen or more with her, and promising to send early the next morning for their trunks. With so many of the fairest damsels secured for a visit of a week or a fortnight, the young hostess was sure of cavaliers in plenty to do her guests honor. And upon my word it was all very pleasant! I have idled away many a week in these old country houses, and for my life I cannot manage to regret the fact, or to remember it with a single pang of remorse for the wasted hours. Perhaps after all they were not wholly wasted. Who shall say? Other things than gold are golden.

As a guest in those houses one was not welcome only, but free. There was a servant to take your horse, a servant to brush your clothes, a servant to attend you whenever you had a want to supply or a wish to gratify. But you were never oppressed with attentions, or under any kind of restraint. If you liked to sit in the parlor, the women there would entertain you very agreeably, or set you to entertaining them by reading aloud, or by anything else which might suggest itself. If you preferred the piazza, there were sure to be others like-minded with yourself. If you smoked, there were always pipes and tobacco on the sideboard, and a man-servant to bring them to you if you were not inclined to go after them. In short, each guest might do precisely as he pleased, sure that in doing so he should best please his host and hostess.

My own favorite amusement—I am the father of a family now, and may freely confess the fancies and foibles of a departed youth—was to accompany the young mistress of the mansion on her rounds of domestic duty, carrying her key-basket for her, and assisting her in various ways, unlocking doors and—really I cannot remember that I was of any very great use to her after all; but willingness counts for a good deal in this world, and I was always very willing at any rate. As a rule, the young daughter of the mansion was housekeeper, and this may perhaps account for the fact that the habit of carrying housekeeper's key-baskets for them was very general among the young gentlemen in houses where they were upon terms of intimate friendship.

Life in Virginia was the pursuit of happiness and its attainment. Money was a means only, and was usually spent very lavishly whenever its expenditure could add in any way to comfort, but as there was never any occasion to spend it for mere display, most of the planters were abundantly able to use it freely for better purposes. That is to say, most of them were able to owe their debts and to renew their notes when necessary. Their houses were built for comfort, and most of them had grown gray with age long before the present generation was born. A great passage-way ran through the middle, commonly, and here stood furniture which would have delighted the heart of the mediaevalist: great, heavy oaken chairs, black with age and polished with long usage—chairs whose joints were naked and not ashamed; sofas of ponderous build, made by carpenters who were skeptical as to the strength of woods, and thought it necessary to employ solid pieces of oak, four inches in diameter, for legs, and to shoe each with a solid brass lion's paw as a precaution against abrasion. A great porch in front was shut out at night by the ponderous double doors of the hallway, but during the day the way was wide open through the house.

The floors were of white ash, and in summer no carpets or rugs were anywhere to be seen. Every morning the floors were polished by diligent scouring with dry pine needles, and the furniture similarly brightened by rubbing with wax and cork. In the parlors the furniture was usually very rich as to woods and very antique in workmanship. The curtains were of crimson damask with lace underneath, and the contrast between these and the bare, white, polished floor was singularly pleasing.

The first white person astir in the house every morning was the woman who carried the keys, mother or daughter, as the case might be. Her morning work was no light affair, and its accomplishment consumed several hours daily. To begin with she must knead the light bread with her own hands and send it to the kitchen to be baked and served hot at breakfast. She must prepare a skillet full of light rolls for the same meal, and "give out" the materials for the rest of the breakfast. Then she must see to the sweeping and garnishing of the lower rooms, passages, and porches, lest the maids engaged in that task should entertain less extreme views than her own on the subject of that purity and cleanliness which constituted the house's charm and the housekeeper's crown of honor. She must write two or three notes, to be dispatched by the hands of a small Negro to her acquaintances in the neighborhood—a kind of correspondence much affected in that society. In the midst of all these duties, the young housekeeper—for somehow it is only the youthful ones whom I remember vividly—must meet and talk with such of the guests as might happen to be early risers, and must not forget to send a messenger to the kitchen once every ten minutes to "hurry up breakfast!" —not that breakfast could be hurried under any conceivable circumstances, but merely because it was the custom to send such messages, and the young woman was a duty-loving maid who did her part in the world without inquiring why. She knew very well that breakfast would be ready at the traditional hour, the hour at which it always had been served in that house, and that there was no power on the plantation great enough to hasten it by a single minute. But she sent out to "hurry" it nevertheless.

When breakfast is ready the guests are ready for it. It is a merit of fixed habits that one can conform to them easily, and when one knows that breakfast has been ready in the house in which he is staying precisely at nine o'clock every morning for one or two centuries past, and that the immovable conservatism of an old Virginian cook stands guard over the sanctity of that custom, he has no difficulty in determining when to begin dressing.

The breakfast is sure to be a good one, consisting of everything obtainable at the season. If it be in summer, the host will have a dish of broiled roe herrings before him, a plate of hot rolls at his right hand, and a cylindrical loaf of hot white bread—which it is his duty to cut and serve—on his left. On the flanks will be one or two plates of beaten biscuit and a loaf of batter bread, *i. e.*, corn-bread made rich with milk and eggs. A dish of plain corn "pones" sits on the dresser, and the servants bring griddle-cakes or waffles hot from the kitchen; so much for breads. A knuckle of cold, boiled ham is always present, on either the table or the dresser, as convenience may dictate. A dish of sliced tomatoes and another of broiled ditto are the invariable vegetables, supplemented on occasion with lettuce, radishes, and other like things. These are the staples of breakfast, and additions are made as the season serves.

Breakfast over, the young housekeeper scalds and dries the dishes and glassware with her own hands. Then she goes to the garden, smoke-house, and store-room, to "give out" for dinner. Morning rides, backgammon, music, reading, etc., furnish amusement until one o'clock, or a little later. The gentlemen go shooting or fishing, if they choose, or join the host in his rides over the plantation, inspecting his corn, tobacco, wheat, and live stock. About one the house grows quiet. The women retire to their chambers, the gentlemen make themselves comfortable in various ways. About two it is the duty of the master of the mansion to offer toddy or juleps to his guests, and to ask one of the dining-room servants if "dinner is 'most ready." Half an hour later he must send the cook word to "hurry it up." It is to be served at four, of course, but as the representative of an ancient house, it is his bounden duty to ask the two-o'clock question and send the half-past-two message.

Supper is served at eight, and the women usually retire for the night at ten or eleven.

If hospitality was deemed the chief of virtues among the Virginians, the duty of accepting hospitality was quite as strongly insisted upon. One must visit his friends, whatever the circumstances, if he would not be thought churlish. Especially were young men required to show a proper respect and affection for elderly female relatives by dining with them as frequently as at any other house. I shall not soon forget some experiences of my own in this regard. The most stately and elegant country-house I have ever seen stood in our neighborhood. Its master had lived in great state there, and after his death his two maiden sisters, left alone in the great mansion, scrupulously maintained every

custom he had established or inherited. They were my
cousins in the Virginian sense of the word, and I had not
been long a resident of the State when my guardian reminded me of my duty toward them. I must ride over and
dine there without a special invitation, and I must do this
six or eight times a year at the least. As a mere boy, half-
grown, I made ready for my visit with a good deal of awe
and trepidation. I had already met the two stately dames
and was disposed to distrust my manners in their presence.
I went, however, and was received with warm, though rather
stiff and formal, cordiality. My horse was taken to the
stable. I was shown to my room by a thoroughly drilled
servant, whose tongue had been trained to as persistent a
silence as if his functions had been those of a mute at a
funeral. His name I discovered was Henry, but beyond this
I could make no progress in his acquaintance. He prided
himself upon knowing his place, and the profound respect
with which he treated me made it impossible that I should
ask him for the information on which my happiness, perhaps my reputation, just then depended. I wanted to know
for what purpose I had been shown to my room, what I was
expected to do there, and at what hour I ought to descend
to the parlor or library.

It was manifestly out of the question to seek such information at the hands of so well-regulated a being as Henry.
He had ushered me into my room and now stood bolt up-
right, gazing fixedly at nothing and waiting for my orders
in profound and immovable silence. He had done his part
well, and it was not for him to assume that I was unpre-
pared to do mine. His attitude indicated, or perhaps I
should say aggressively asserted, the necessity he was under
of assuming my entire familiarity with the usages of good
society and the ancient customs of this ancient house. The
worst of it was I fancied that the solemn rogue guessed my

ignorance and delighted in exposing my fraudulent pretensions to good breeding. But in this I did him an injustice, as future knowledge of him taught me. He was well drilled, and delighted in doing his duty, that was all. No *gaucherie* on my part would have moved him to smile. He knew his place and his business too well for that. Whatever I might have done he would have held to be perfectly proper. It was for him to stand there like a statue, until I should bid him do otherwise, and if I had kept him there for a week I think he would have given no sign of weariness or impatience. As it was, his presence appalled and oppressed me, and in despair of discovering the proper thing to do, I determined to put a bold face upon the matter.

"I am tired and warm," I said, "and will rest awhile upon the bed. I will join the ladies in half an hour. You may go now."

At dinner, Henry stood at the sideboard and silently directed the servants. When the cloth was removed, he brought a wine tub with perhaps a dozen bottles of antique Madeira in it and silently awaited my signal before decanting one of them. When I had drunk a glass with the ladies, they rose and retired according to the custom, leaving me alone with the wine and the cigars—and Henry, whose erect solemnity converted the great silent dining-room into something very like a funeral chamber. He stood there like a guardsman on duty, immovable, speechless, patient, while I sat at the board, a decanter of wine before me and the tub of unopened bottles on the floor by my side—enough for a regiment.

I did not want any wine or anything else except a sound of some sort to break the horrible stillness. I tried to think of some device by which to make Henry go out of the room or move one of his hands or turn his eyes a little or even wink; but I failed utterly. There was nothing whatever to be done. There was no order to give him. Every want was supplied and everything was at my hand. The cigars were under my nose, the ash pan by them, and a lighted wax candle stood within reach. I toyed with the decanter in the hope of breaking the stillness, but its stand was too well cushioned above and below to make a sound. I ventured at last to move one of my feet, but a strip of velvet carpet lay between it and the floor.

I could stand it no longer. Filling a glass of wine I drank it off, lighted a fresh cigar, and boldly strode out of the house to walk on the lawn in front.

On the occasion of subsequent visits I got on well enough, knowing precisely what to expect and what to do, and in time I came to regard this as one of the very pleasantest houses in which I visited at all, if on no other account than because I found myself perfectly free there to do as I pleased; but until I learned that I was expected to consult only my own comfort while a guest in the house the atmosphere of the place oppressed me.

Not in every house were the servants so well trained as Henry, but what they lacked in skill they fully made up in numbers, and in hardly anything else was the extravagance of the Virginians so manifest as in their wastefulness of labor. On nearly every plantation there were ten or twelve able-bodied men and women employed about the house, doing the work which two or three ought to have done, and might have done; and in addition to this there were usually a dozen or a score of others with merely nominal duties or no duties at all. But it was useless to urge their master to send any of them to the field, and idle to show him that the addition which might thus be made to the force of productive laborers would so increase his revenue as to acquit him of debt within a few years. He did not much care to be free of debt for one thing, and he liked to have plenty of servants always within call. As his dinner table bore every day food enough for a battalion, so his nature demanded the presence of half a dozen servitors whenever one was wanted. Indeed, these people usually summoned servants in squads, calling three or four to take one guest's horse to the stable or to bring one pitcher of ice water.

And yet I should do the Virginians great injustice were I to leave the impression that they were lazy. With abundant possessions, superabundant household help and slave labor, they had a good deal of leisure, but they were nevertheless very industrious people in their way. It was no light undertaking to manage a great plantation and at the same time fulfil the large measure of duties to friends and neighbors which custom imposed. One must visit and receive visitors, and must go to court every month, and to all planters' meetings. Besides this there was a certain amount of fox hunting and squirrel and bird and turkey shooting and fishing to be done, from which it was really very difficult to escape with any credit to oneself. On the whole, the time of the planters was pretty fully occupied. The women had household duties, and these included the cutting and making of clothes for all the Negroes on the plantation, a heavy task which might as well have been done by the Negro seamstresses, except that such was not the custom. Fair women who kept dressmakers for themselves worked day after day on coarse cloths, manufacturing coats and trousers for the field hands. They did a great deal of embroidery and worsted work too, and personally instructed Negro girls in the use of the needle and scissors. All this, with their necessary visiting and entertaining, and their daily attendance upon the sick Negroes, whom they always visited and cared for in person, served to make the Virginian women about the busiest women I have ever known. Even Sunday brought them little rest, for, in addition to other duties on that day, each of them spent some hours at the "quarters" holding a Sunday-school.

Nevertheless the Virginians had a good deal of leisure on their hands, and their command of time was a very important agent, I should say, in the formation of their characters as individuals, and as a people. It bred habits of out-door exercise, which gave the young men stalwart frames and robust constitutions. It gave form to their social life. Above all, it made reading men and students of many, though their reading and their study were of a somewhat peculiar kind. They were all Latinists, inasmuch as Latin formed the staple of their ordinary school course. It was begun early and continued to the end, and even in after life very many planters were in the habit of reading their Virgil and their Horace and their Ovid as an amusement, so that it came to be assumed, quite as a matter of course, that every gentleman with any pretension to culture could read Latin easily, and quote Horace and Juvenal from memory.

But they read English literature still more largely, and in no part of the country, except in distinctly literary centres like Cambridge or Concord, are really rich house-hold libraries so common a possession, I think, as they were among the best classes of Virginian planters. Let us open the old glass doors and see what books the Virginians read. The libraries in the old houses were the growth of many generations, begun perhaps by the English cadet who founded the family on this side of the water in the middle of the seventeenth century, and added to little by little from that day to this. They were especially rich in the English classics, in early editions with long *s's* and looped *ct's,* but sadly deficient in the literature of the present. In one of them, I remember, I found nearly everything from Chaucer to Byron, and comparatively little that was later. From

Pope to Southey it furnished a pretty complete geologic section of English literature, and from internal evidence I conclude that when the founder of the family and the library first took up his residence in the Old Dominion, Swift was still a contributor to the *Gentleman's Magazine,* and Pope was a poet not many years dead.

There was a copy of *Tom Jones,* and another of *Joseph Andrews,* printed in Fielding's own time. The *Spectator* was there, not in the shape of a reprint, but the original papers, rudely bound, a treasure brought from England, doubtless, by the immigrant. Richardson, Smollett, Swift, and the rest were present in contemporary editions; the poets and essayists, pretty much all of them, in quaint old volumes; Johnson's *Lives of the Poets;* Sheridan's plays, stitched; Burke's works; Scott's novels in force, just as they came, one after another, from the press of the Edinburgh publishers; Miss Edgeworth's moralities elbowing Mrs. Aphra Behn's strongly tainted romances; Miss Burney's *Evelina,* which was so "proper" that all the young ladies used to read it, but so dull that nobody ever opens it nowadays; and scores of other old "new books," which I have no room to catalogue here, even if I could remember them all.

Byron appeared, not as a whole, but in separate volumes, bought as each was published. Even the poor little *Hours of Idleness* was there, ordered from across the sea, doubtless, in consequence of the savage treatment it received at the hands of the *Edinburgh Review,* bound volumes of which were on the shelves below. There was no copy of "English Bards and Scotch Reviewers," but as nearly all the rest of Byron's poems were there in original editions, it seems probable that the satire also had once held a place in the library. It had been read to pieces, perhaps, or borrowed and never returned.

There were histories of all kinds, and collected editions of standard works in plenty, covering a wide field of law, politics, theology, and what not.

Of strictly modern books the assortment was comparatively meagre. Macaulay's *Miscellanies,* Motley's *Dutch Republic,* Prescott's *Mexico, Peru,* etc.; stray volumes of Dickens, Thackeray, Bulwer, and Lever; Kennedy's *Swallow Barn,* Cooke's *Virginia Comedians,* half a dozen volumes of Irving, and a few others made up the list.

Of modern poetry there was not a line, and in this, as in other respects, the old library—burned during the war— fairly represented the literary tastes and reading habits of the Virginians in general. They read little or no recent poetry and not much recent prose. I think this was not so much the result of prejudice as of education. The schools in Virginia were excellent ones of their kind, but their system was that of a century ago. They gave attention chiefly to "the humanities" and logic, and the education of a Virginian gentleman resembled that of an Englishman of the last century far more closely than that of any modern American. The writers of the present naturally address themselves to men of to-day, and this is precisely what the Virginians were not, wherefore modern literature was not at all a thing to their taste.

To all this there were of course exceptions. I have known some Virginians who appreciated Tennyson, enjoyed Longfellow and Lowell, and understood Browning; just as I have known a few who affected a modern pronunciation of the letter "a" in such words as "master," "basket," "glass," and "grass."

CHAPTER 2

THE MUSTERING

———————◄●►———————

THAT was an admirable idea of De Quincey's, formally to postulate any startling theory upon which he desired to build an argument or a story, and to insist that his readers should regard the postulate as proved, on pain of losing altogether what he had to say. The plan is a very convenient one, saving a deal of argument, and establishing in the outset a very desirable relation of mastery and subordination between writer and reader. Indeed, but for some such device I should never be able to get on at all with these sketches, fully to understand which, the reader must make of himself, for the time at least, a Confederate. He must put himself in the place of the Southerners and look at some things through their eyes, if he would understand those things and their results at all; and as it is no part of my purpose to write a defense of the Southern view of any question, it will save a good deal of explanation on my part, and weariness on the part of the reader, if I follow De Quincey's example and do a little postulating to begin with. I shall make no attempt whatever to prove my postulates, but any one interested in these pages will find it to his advantage to accept them, one and all, as proved, pending the reading of what is to follow. After that he may relapse as speedily as he pleases into his own opinions. Here are the postulates:

1. The Southerners honestly believed in the right of secession, not merely as a revolutionary, but as a constitutional right. They not only held that whenever any people finds the government under which it is living oppressive and subversive of the ends for which it was instituted, it is both the right and the duty of that people to throw off the government and establish a new one in its stead; but they believed also that every State in the Union held the reserved right, under the constitution, to withdraw peaceably from the Union at pleasure.

2. They believed that every man's allegiance was due to his State only, and that it was only by virtue of the State's continuance in the Union that any allegiance was due to the general government at all; wherefore the withdrawal of a State from the Union would of itself absolve all the citizens of that State from whatever obligations they were under to maintain and respect the Federal constitution. In other words, patriotism, as the South understood it, meant devotion to one's State, and only a secondary and consequential devotion to the Union, existing as a result of the State's action in making itself a part of the Union, and terminable at any time by the State's withdrawal.

3. They were as truly and purely patriotic in their secession and in the fighting which followed, as were the people of the North in their adherence to the Union itself. The difference was one of opinion as to what the duties of a patriot were, and not at all a difference in the degree of patriotism existing in the two sections.

4. You, reader, who shouldered your musket and fought like the hero you are, for the Union and the old flag, if you had been bred at the South, and had understood your duty

as the Southerners did theirs, would have fought quite as bravely for secession as you did against it; and you would have been quite as truly a hero in the one case as in the other, because in either you would have risked your life for the sake of that which you held to be the right. If the reader will bear all this in mind we shall get on much better than we otherwise could, in our effort to catch a glimpse of the war from a Southern point of view.

With all its horrors and in spite of the wretchedness it has wrought, this war of ours, in some of its aspects at least, begins to look like a very ridiculous affair, now that we are getting too far away from it to hear the rattle of the musketry; and I have a mind, in this chapter, to review one of its most ridiculous phases, to wit, its beginning. We all remember Mr. Webster's pithy putting of the case with regard to our forefathers of a hundred years ago: "They went to war against a preamble. They fought seven years against a declaration. They poured out their treasures and their blood like water, in a contest in opposition to an assertion." Now it seems to me that something very much like this might be said of the Southerners, and particularly of the Virginians, without whose pluck and pith there could have been no war at all worth writing or talking about. They made war upon a catch-word, and fought until they were hopelessly ruined for the sake of an abstraction. And certainly history will not find it to the discredit of those people that they freely offered themselves upon the altar of an abstract principle of right, in a war which they knew must work hopeless ruin to themselves, whatever its other results might be. Virginia did not want to secede, and her decision to this effect was given in the election of a convention composed for the most part of men strongly opposed to secession. The Virginians believed they had both a moral and a constitutional right to withdraw voluntarily from a Union into which they had voluntarily gone, but the majority of them preferred to remain as they were. They did not feel themselves particularly aggrieved or threatened by the election of Mr. Lincoln, and so, while they never doubted that they had an unquestionable right to secede at will, they decided by their votes not to do anything of the kind. This decision was given in the most unmistakable way, by heavy majorities, in an election which involved no other issue whatever. But without Virginia the States which had already passed ordinances of secession would have been wholly unable to sustain themselves. Virginia's strength in men, material, and geographical position was very necessary, for one thing, and her moral influence on North Carolina, Arkansas, and other hesitating States, was even more essential to the success of the movement. Accordingly every possible effort was made to ''fire the heart'' of the conservative old commonwealth. Delegations, with ponderous stump speeches in their mouths and parchment appeals in their hands, were sent from the seceding States to Richmond, while every Virginian who actively favored secession was constituted a committee of one to cultivate a public sentiment in favor of the movement.

Then came such a deluge of stump speeches as would have been impossible in any other state or country in the civilized world, for there never yet was a Virginian who could not, on occasion, acquit himself very well on the hustings. The process of getting up the requisite amount of enthusiasm, in the country districts especially, was in many cases a very laughable one. In one county, I remember, the principal speakers were three lawyers of no very great weight except in a time of excitement. One of them was colonel of the county militia, another liteutenant-colonel, and the third captain of a troop of volunteer cavalry, a fine body of men, who spent three or four days of each month

partly in practicing a system of drill which, I am persuaded, is as yet wholly undreamed of by any of the writers
upon tactics, and partly in cultivating the social virtues
over that peculiar species of feast known as a barbecue.
When it became evident that the people of Virginia were
not duly impressed with the wrong done them in the election
of Mr. Lincoln, these were unquestionably the right men in
the right places. They were especially fond of fervid speech-
making, and not one of them had ever been known to neglect
an opportunity to practice it; each could make a speech on
any subject at a moment's warning. They spoke quite as
well on a poor theme as on a good one, and it was even
claimed for one of them that his eloquence waxed hottest
when he had no subject at all to talk about. Here, then, was
their opportunity. The ever-full vials of their eloquence
waited only for the uncorking. It was the rule of their lives
to make a speech wherever and whenever they could get an
audience, and under the militia law they could, at will,
compel the attendance of a body of listeners consisting of
pretty nearly all the voters of the county, plus the small
boys. When they were big with speech they had only to
order a drill. If a new gush of words or a felicitous illustration occurred to them overnight, they called a general
muster for the next day. Two of them were candidates,
against a quiet and sensible planter, for the one seat allowed
the county in the convention, and the only difference of
opinion there was between them was involved in the question whether the ordinance of secession should be adopted
before or after breakfast on the morning of the first day of
the convention's existence. One wanted coffee first and the
other did not. On the day of election, a drunken fellow,
without a thought of saying a good thing, apologized to one
of them for not having voted for him, saying, ''I promised
you, Sam—but I couldn't do it. You're a good fellow, Sam,

and smart at a speech, but you see, Sam, you *haven't the weight o' head.*'' The people, as the result of the election showed, entertained a like view of the matter, and the lawyers were both beaten by the old planter.

It was not until after the convention assembled, however, that the eloquence of the triad came into full play. They then labored unceasingly to find words with which to express their humiliation in view of the degeneracy and cowardice of the ancient commonwealth.

They rejoiced in the thought that sooner or later the People—which they always pronounced with an uncommonly big P—would ''hurl those degenerate sons of illustrious sires,'' meaning thereby the gentlemen who had been elected to the convention, ''from the seats which they were now polluting,'' and a good deal more of a similar sort, the point of which was that these orators longed for war of the bloodiest kind, and were happy in the belief that it would come, in spite of the fact that the convention was overwhelmingly against secession.

Now, in view of the subsequent history of these belligerent orators, it would be a very interesting thing to know just what they thought a war between the sections promised. One of them, as I have said, was colonel of the two or three hundred militia-men mustered in the county. Another was lieutenant-colonel, and the third was captain of a volunteer troop, organized under the militia law for purposes of amusement, chiefly. This last one could, of course, retain his rank, should his company be mustered into service, and the other two firmly believed that they would be called into camp as full-fledged field-officers. In view of this, the colonel, in one of his speeches, urged upon his men the necessity of a rigid self-examination, touching the matter of personal courage, before going, in his regiment, to the battle-field; ''For,'' said he, ''where G. leads, brave men must follow,'' a bit of rhetoric which brought down the house as a matter of course. The others were equally valiant in anticipation of war and equally eager for its coming; and yet when the war did come, so sorely taxing the resources of the South as to make a levy *en masse* necessary, not one of the three ever managed to hear the whistle of a bullet. The colonel did indeed go as far as Richmond, during the spring of 1861, but discovering there that he was physically unfit for service, went no farther. The lieutenant-colonel ran away from the field while the battle was yet afar off, and the captain, suffering from "nervous prostration," sent in his resignation, which was unanimously accepted by his men, on the field during the first battle of Bull Run.

I sketch these three men and their military careers not without a purpose. They serve to correct an error. They were types of a class which brought upon the South a deal of odium. Noisy speech-makers, they were too often believed by strangers to be, as they pretended, representative men, and their bragging, their intolerance, their contempt for the North, their arrogance—all these were commonly laid to the charge of the Southern people as a whole. As a matter of fact, these were not representative men at all. They assumed the *rôle* of leadership on the court-house greens, but were repudiated by the people at the polls first, and afterwards when the volunteers were choosing officers to command them in actual warfare. These men were clamorous demagogues and nothing else. They had no influence whatever upon the real people. Their vaporings were applauded and laughed at. The applause was ridicule, and the laughter was closely akin to jeering.

Meantime a terrible dread was brooding over the minds of the Virginian people. They were brave men and patriots, who would maintain their honor at any cost. They were ready to sacrifice their lives and their treasures in a hopeless struggle about an abstraction, should the time come when their sense of right and honor required the sacrifice at their hands. There was no cowardice and no hesitation to be expected of them when the call should come. But they dreaded war, and most of them prayed that it might never be. They saw only desolation in its face. They knew it would lay waste their fields and bring want upon their families, however it might result in regard to the great political questions involved in it. And so they refused to go headlong into a war which meant for them destruction. Some of them, believing that there was no possibility of avoiding the struggle, thought it the part of wisdom to accept the inevitable and begin hostilities at once, while the North was still but poorly prepared for aggressive measures. But the majority of the Virginians were disposed to wait and to avoid war altogether, if that should prove possible. These said, "We should remain quiet until some overt act of hostility shall make resistance necessary." And these were called cowards and fogies by the brave men of the hustings already alluded to.

There was still another class of men who were opposed to secession in any case. Of these, William C. Wickham, of Hanover, and Jubal Early will serve as examples. They thought secession unnecessary and imprudent in any conceivable event. They believed that it offered no remedy for existing or possible ills, and that it could result only in the prostration of the South. They opposed it, therefore, with all their might; not only as not yet called for, but as suicidal in any event, and not to be thought of at all. And yet these men, when the war came, believed it to be their duty to side with their State, and fought so manfully in behalf of the South as to make themselves famous military leaders.

Why, then, the reader doubtless asks, if this was the temper of the Virginians, did Virginia secede after all? I answer, because circumstances ultimately so placed the Virginians that they could not, without cowardice and dishonor, do otherwise ; and the Virginians are brave men and honorable ones. They believed, as I have said, in the abstract right of any State to secede at will. Indeed, this right was to them as wholly unquestioned and unquestionable as is the right of the States to establish free schools, or to do any other thing pertaining to local self-government. The question of the correctness or incorrectness of the doctrine is not now to the purpose. The Virginians, almost without an exception, believed and had always believed it absolutely, and believing it, they held of necessity that the general government had no right, legal or moral, to coerce a seceding State ; and so, when the President called upon Virginia for her quota of troops with which to compel the return of the seceding States, she could not possibly obey without doing that which her people believed to be an outrage upon the rights of sister commonwealths, for which, as they held, there was no warrant in law or equity.

She heartily condemned the secession of South Carolina and the rest as unnecessary, ill-advised, and dangerous ; but their secession did not concern her except as a looker-on, and she had not only refused to be a partaker in it, but had also felt a good deal of indignation against the men who were thus endangering the peace of the land. When she was called upon to assist in reducing these States to submission, however, she could no longer remain a spectator. She must furnish the troops, and so assist in doing that which she believed to be utterly wrong, or she must herself withdraw from the Union. The question was thus narrowed down to this : Should Virginia seek safety in dishonor, or should she meet destruction in doing that which she believed to be right ? Such a question was not long to be debated. Two days after the proclamation was published Virginia seceded, not because she wanted to secede—not because she believed it wise—but because, as she understood the matter, the only other course open to her would have been cowardly and dishonorable.

Now, unless I am sadly mistaken, the Virginians understood what secession implied much more perfectly than did the rest of the Southern people. They anticipated no child's play, and having cast in their lot with the South, they began at once to get ready for war. From one end of the State to the other, every county seat became a drill field. The courts suspended their sessions, on the ground that it was not a proper time for the enforced collection of debts. Volunteer companies soon drained the militia organization of its men. Public opinion said that every man who did not embrace the very surest and earliest opportunity of getting himself mustered into actual service was a coward; and so, to withdraw from the militia and join a volunteer company, and make a formal tender of services to the State, became absolutely essential to the maintenance of one's reputation as a gentleman.

The drilling, of which there was literally no end, was simply funny. Maneuvers of the most utterly impossible sort were carefully taught to the men. Every amateur officer had his own pet system of tactics, and the effect of the incongruous teachings, when brought out in battalion drill, closely resembled that of the music at Mr. Bob Sawyer's party, where each guest sang the chorus to the tune he knew best.

The militia colonels, having assumed a sort of general authority over the volunteer companies which had been formed out of the old militia material, were not satisfied with daily musterings of the men under their captains— musterings which left the field-officers nothing to do—and so in a good many of the counties they ordered all the men into camp at the county seat, and drew upon the people for provisions with which to feed them. The camps were irregular, disorderly affairs, over which no rod of discipline could very well be held, as the men were not legally soldiers, and the only punishment possible for disobedience or neglect of duty was a small fine, which the willful men, with true Virginian contempt for money in small sums, paid cheerfully as a tax upon jollity.

The camping, however, was enjoyable in itself, and as most of the men had nothing else to do, the attendance upon roll-call was a pretty full one. Every man brought a servant or two with him, of course. How else were his boots and his accouterments to be kept clean, his horse to be groomed, and his meals cooked? Most of the ladies came, too, in their carriages every morning, returning to their homes only as night came on; and so the camps were very picturesque and very delightful places to be in. All the men wore epaulets of a gorgeousness rarely equaled except in portraits of field-marshals, and every man was a hero in immediate prospect.

One day an alarming report came, to the effect that a little transport steamer, well known in James River, was on her way up to Richmond with ten thousand troops on board, and instantly the camps at the court-houses along the railroads were astir. It entered into nobody's head to inquire where so many troops could have come from at a time when the entire active force of the United States army from Maine to Oregon was hardly greater than that; nor did anybody seem surprised that the whole ten thousand had managed to bestow themselves on board a steamer the carrying capacity of which had hitherto been about four or five hundred men. The report was accepted as true, and everybody believed that the ten thousand men would be poured into Richmond's defenseless streets within an hour or two. In the particular county to which I have alluded in the beginning of this chapter, the cavalry captain sent for half a dozen grindstones, and set his men to grinding their sabres —a process which utterly ruined the blades, of course. The militia colonel telegraphed a stump speech or two to Richmond, which did no particular harm, as the old station agent who officiated as operator could not for his life send a message of more than three words so that it could be read at the other end of the line. A little telegraphic swearing came back over the wires, but beyond that the colonel's glowing messages resulted in nothing. Turning his attention to matters more immediately within his control, therefore, he ordered the drums to beat, and assembling the men he marched them boldly down to the railroad station, where mounting a goods box he told them that the time for speechmaking was now past; that the enemy (I am not sure that he did not say "vandal," and make some parenthetical remarks about "Attila flags" and things of that sort which were favorites with him) was now at our very thresholds; that he (the colonel) had marched his command to the depot in answer to the call of his country; that they would proceed thence by rail to Richmond and at once encounter the enemy, etc., etc., etc. He had already telegraphed, he said, to General Lee and to Governor Letcher, requesting them to dispatch a train (the colonel would have scorned to say "send cars" even in a telegram), and the iron horse was doubtless already on its way.

No train came, however, and after nightfall the men were marched back to their quarters in the court-house.

A few days later some genuine orders came from Richmond, accepting the proffered services of all the companies organized in the county, and ordering all, except the one cavalry troop, into camp at Richmond. These orders, by some strange oversight, the colonel explained, were addressed, not to him as colonel, but to the several captains individually. He was not disposed to stand on ceremony, however, he said; and so, without waiting for the clerical error to be rectified, he would comply with the spirit of the order, and take the troops to Richmond as soon as the necessary transportation should arrive. Transportation was a good, mouth-filling word, which suited the colonel exactly. In order that there should be no delay or miscarriage, he marched the men a hundred yards down the hill to the station, ten hours in advance of the time at which the cars were to be there; and as there was nothing else to do, he and his lieutenant thought the occasion a good one for the making of a speech apiece. The colonel expressed his hearty sympathy with the woes of the cavalry, who were to be left at home, while the infantry was winning renown. And yet, he said, he had expected this from the first. The time had been, he explained, when the cavalry was the quick-moving arm of the service, but now that the iron horse. . . . The reader must imagine the rest of that grandiloquent sentence. I value my reputation for veracity too much to risk it by following the colonel in this, his supreme burst of impassioned oratory. He was sorry for the cavalry, but they should console themselves with the thought that, as preservers of order in the community and protectors of their homes, they would not be wholly useless in their own humble way; and should any of them visit the army, they would always meet a hearty welcome in his camp. For the present his headquarters would be in the Spottswood Hotel, and he would be glad, whenever military duty did not too greatly absorb his attention, to grasp the hand of any member of the troop who, wishing to catch a glimpse of real warfare, should seek him there.

The train came, after a while, and the unappreciative railroad men obstinately insisted that the State paid for the passage of certain designated companies only, and that these distinguished field-officers, if they traveled by that train at all, must pay their way at regular passenger rates. The colonel and his lieutenant pocketed the insult and paid their fare; but when, upon the arrival of the troops at Richmond, nobody seemed to know anything about these field-officers, and the companies were sent, without them, into camps of instruction, the gallant leaders returned by passenger train to their homes. The colonel came back, he said in a speech at the station, still further to stir the patriotism of the people. He had been in consultation with the authorities in Richmond; and while it would not be proper for him to reveal even to these, his patriotic countrymen, the full plan of campaign confided to him as a field-officer, he might at least say to them that the government, within ten days, would have fifteen thousand men in line on the Potomac, and then, with perchance a bloody but very brief struggle, this overwhelming force would dictate terms to the tyrants at Washington.

This time the colonel got himself unmistakably laughed at, and, so far as I have heard, he made no more speeches.

Meantime it had become evident to everybody that a very real and a very terrible war was in prospect, and there was no longer any disposition to tolerate nonsense of the sort I have been describing. As fast as arrangements could be made for their accommodation, the volunteers from every part of the State were ordered into camps of instruction at Richmond and Ashland. As soon as any company was deemed fit for service, it was sent to the front and assigned to a regiment. Troops from other States were constantly pouring into Richmond, and marching thence to the armies which were forming in the field. The speech-making was over forever, and the work of the war had begun.

CHAPTER 3

THE MEN WHO MADE THE ARMY

A NEWSPAPER correspondent has told us that the great
leader of the German armies, Count Von Moltke, has
never read anything—even a history—of our war,
and that when questioned on the subject, he has said he
could not afford to spend time over "the wrangling of two
armed mobs." If he ever said anything of the kind, which
is doubtful, his characterization of the two armies had reference, probably, to their condition during the first year or
two of the struggle, when they could lay very little claim
indeed to any more distinctively military title. The Southern army, at any rate, was simply a vast mob of rather ill-
armed young gentlemen from the country.[1] As I have said

---

[1] In order that no reader may misconceive the spirit in which this
chapter is written, I wish to say, at the outset, that in commenting
upon the material of which the Southern army was made up, nothing
has been further from my thought than to reflect, even by implication,
upon the character of the Union army or of the men who composed
it, for indeed I honor both as highly as anybody can. I think I have
outlived whatever war prejudices I may have brought with me out of
the struggle, and in writing of some of the better characteristics of
the early Virginian volunteers, I certainly have not meant to deny
equal or like excellence to their foemen. I happen, however, to know a
great deal about the one army and very little about the other,—a state
of things consequent upon the peculiar warmth with which we were
always greeted whenever we undertook to visit the camps of our

in a previous chapter, every gentleman in Virginia, not wholly incapable of rendering service, enlisted at the beginning of the war, and the companies, unarmed, untrained, and hardly even organized, were sent at once to camps of instruction. Here they were in theory drilled and disciplined and made into soldiers, by the little handful of available West-Pointers and the lads from the Military Institute at Lexington. In point of fact, they were only organized and taught the rudiments of the drill before being sent to the front as full-fledged soldiers; and it was only after a year or more of active service in the field that they began to suspect what the real work and the real character of the modern soldier is.

Our ideas of the life and business of a soldier were drawn chiefly from the adventures of Ivanhoe and Charles O'Malley, two worthies with whose personal history almost every man in the army was familiar. The men who volunteered went to war of their own accord, and were wholly unaccustomed to acting on any other than their own motion. They were hardy lovers of field sports, accustomed to out-door life, and in all physical respects excellent material of which to make an army. But they were not used to control of any sort, and were not disposed to obey anybody except for good and sufficient reason given. While actually on drill they obeyed the word of command, not so much by reason of its being proper to obey a command, as because obedience was in that case necessary to the successful issue of a pretty

---

friends on the other side. Will the reader please bear in mind, then, that my estimate of the character of the Southern troops is a positive and not a comparative one, and that nothing said in praise of the one army is meant to be a reflection upon the other? Between Bull Run and Appomattox I had ample opportunity to learn respect for the courage and manliness of the men who overcame us, and since the close of the war I have learned to know many of them as tried and true friends, and gentlemen of noblest mold.

performance in which they were interested. Off drill they did as they pleased, holding themselves gentlemen, and as such bound to consult only their own wills. Their officers were of themselves, chosen by election, and subject, by custom, to enforced resignation upon petition of the men. Only corporals cared sufficiently little for their position to risk any magnifying of their office by the enforcement of discipline. I make of them an honorable exception, out of regard for the sturdy corporal who, at Ashland, marched six of us (a guard detail) through the very middle of a puddle, assigning as his reason for doing so the fact that "It's plagued little authority they give us corporals, and I mean to use that little, any how." Even corporals were elected, however, and until December, 1861, I never knew a single instance in which a captain dared offend his men by breaking a noncommissioned officer, or appointing one, without submitting the matter to a vote of the company. In that first instance the captain had to bolster himself up with written authority from head-quarters, and even then it required three weeks of mingled diplomacy and discipline to quell the mutiny which resulted.

With troops of this kind, the reader will readily understand, a feeling of very democratic equality prevailed, so far at least as military rank had anything to do with it. Officers were no better than men, and so officers and men messed and slept together on terms of entire equality, quarreling and even fighting now and then, in a gentlemanly way, but without a thought of allowing differences of military rank to have any influence in the matter. The theory was that the officers were the creatures of the men, chosen by election to represent their constituency in the performance of certain duties, and that only during good behavior. And to this theory the officers themselves gave in their adhesion in a hundred ways. Indeed, they could do nothing else, inasmuch as they knew no way of quelling a mutiny.

There was one sort of rank, however, which was both maintained and respected from the first, namely, that of social life. The line of demarkation between gentry and common people is not more sharply drawn anywhere than in Virginia. It rests there upon an indeterminate something or other, known as family. To come of a good family is a patent of nobility, and there is no other way whatever by which any man or any woman can find a passage into the charmed circle of Virginia's peerage. There is no college of heralds, to be sure, to which doubtful cases may be referred, and there is no law governing the matter; but every Virginian knows what families are, and what are not good ones, and so mistakes are impossible. The social position of every man is sharply defined, and every man carried it with him into the army. The man of good family felt himself superior, as in most cases he unquestionably was, to his fellow-soldier of less excellent birth; and this distinction was sufficient, during the early years of the war, to override everything like military rank. In one instance which I remember, a young private asserted his superiority of social standing so effectually as to extort from the lieutenant commanding his company a public apology for an insult offered in the subjection of the private to double duty, as a punishment for absence from roll-call. The lieutenant was brave enough to have taken a flogging at the hands of the insulted private, perhaps, but he could not face the declared sentiment of the entire company, and so he apologized. I have known numberless cases in which privates have declined dinner and other invitations from officers who had presumed upon their shoulder-straps in asking the company of their social superiors.

In the camp of instruction at Ashland, where the various cavalry companies existing in Virginia were sent to be made into soldiers, it was a very common thing indeed for men who grew tired of camp fare to take their meals at the hotel, and one or two of them rented cottages and brought their families there, excusing themselves from attendance upon unreasonably early roll-calls, by pleading the distance from their cottages to the parade-ground. Whenever a detail was made for the purpose of cleaning the camp-ground, the men detailed regarded themselves as responsible for the proper performance of the task by their servants, and uncomplainingly took upon themselves the duty of sitting on the fence and superintending the work. The two or three men of the overseer class who were to be found in nearly every company turned some nimble quarters by standing other men's turns of guard-duty at twenty-five cents an hour; and one young gentleman of my own company, finding himself assigned to a picket rope post, where his only duty was to guard the horses and prevent them, in their untrained exuberance of spirit, from becoming entangled in each other's heels and halters, coolly called his servant and turned the matter over to him, with a rather informal but decidedly pointed injunction not to let those horses get themselves into trouble if he valued his hide. This case coming to the ears of Colonel (afterwards General) Ewell, who was commanding the camp, that officer reorganized the guard service upon principles as novel as they were objectionable to the men. He required the men to stand their own turns, and, worse than that, introduced the system, in vogue among regular troops, of keeping the entire guard detail at the guard-house when not on post, an encroachment upon personal liberty which sorely tried the patience of the young cavaliers.

It was in this undisciplined state that the men who afterwards made up the army under Lee were sent to the field to meet the enemy at Bull Run and elsewhere, and the only wonder is that they were ever able to fight at all. They were certainly not soldiers. They were as ignorant of the alphabet of obedience as their officers were of the art of commanding. And yet they acquitted themselves reasonably well, a fact which can be explained only by reference to the causes of their insubordination in camp. These men were the people of the South, and the war was their own; wherefore they fought to win it of their own accord, and not at all because their officers commanded them to do so. Their personal spirit and their intelligence were their sole elements of strength. Death has few terrors for such men, as compared with dishonor, and so they needed no officers at all, and no discipline, to insure their personal good conduct on the field of battle. The same elements of character, too, made them accept hardship with the utmost cheerfulness, as soon as hardship became a necessary condition to the successful prosecution of a war that every man of them regarded as his own. In camp, at Richmond or Ashland, they had shunned all unnecessary privation and all distasteful duty, because they then saw no occasion to endure avoidable discomfort. But in the field they showed themselves great, stalwart men in spirit as well as in bodily frame, and endured cheerfully the hardships of campaigning precisely as they would have borne the fatigues of a hunt, as incidents encountered in the prosecution of their purposes.

During the spring and early summer of 1861, the men did not dream that they were to be paid anything for their services, or even that the government was to clothe them. They had bought their own uniforms, and whenever these wore out they ordered new ones to be sent, by the first opportunity, from home. I remember the very first time the thought of getting clothing from the government ever entered my own mind. I was serving in Stuart's cavalry, and the summer of 1861 was nearly over. My boots had worn out, and as there happened at the time to be a strict embargo upon all visiting on the part of non-military people, I could not get a new pair from home. The spurs of my comrades had made uncomfortable impressions upon my bare feet every day for a week, when some one suggested that I might possibly buy a pair of boots from the quartermaster, who was for the first time in possession of some government property of that description. When I returned with the boots and reported that the official had refused my proffered cash, contenting himself with charging the amount against me as a debit to be deducted from the amount of my *pay and clothing allowance,* there was great merriment in the camp. The idea that there was anybody back of us in this war—anybody who could, by any ingenuity of legal quibbling, be supposed to be indebted to us for our voluntary services in our own cause—was too ridiculous to be treated seriously. "Pay money" became the standing subject for jests. The card-playing with which the men amused themselves suffered a revolution at once; euchre gave place to poker, played for "pay money," the winnings to fall due when pay-day should come—a huge joke which was heartily enjoyed.

From this the reader will see how little was done in the beginning of the war toward the organization of an efficient quartermaster's department, and how completely this ill-organized and undisciplined mob of plucky gentlemen was left to prosecute the war as best it could, trusting to luck for clothing and even for food. Of these things I shall have occasion to speak more fully in a future chapter, wherein I shall have something to say of the management of affairs at Richmond. At present, I merely refer to the matter for the purpose of correcting an error (if I may hope to do that) which seems likely to creep into history. We have been told over and over again that the Confederate army could not possibly have given effectual pursuit to General McDowell's flying forces after the battle of Bull Run. It is urged, in defense of the inaction which made of that day's work a waste effort, that we could not move forward for want of transportation and supplies. Now, without discussing the question whether or not a prompt movement on Washington would have resulted favorably to the Confederates, I am certain, as every man who was there is, that this want of transportation and supplies had nothing whatever to do with it. We had no supplies of any importance, it is true, but none were coming to us there, and we were no whit better off in this regard at Manassas than we would have been before Washington. And having nothing to transport, we needed no transportation. Had the inefficiency of the supply department stopped short at its failure to furnish wagon trains, it might have stood in the way of a forward movement. But that was no ordinary incompetence which governed this department of our service in all its ramifications. The breadth and comprehensiveness of that incompetence were its distinguishing characteristics. In failing to furnish anything to transport, it neutralized its failure to furnish transportation, and the army that fought at Bull Run would have been as well off anywhere else as there, during the next ten days. Indeed, two days after the battle we were literally starved out at Manassas, and were forced to advance to Fairfax Court House in order to get the supplies which the Union army had left in abundance wherever there was a storing-place for them. The next morning after the battle, many of the starving men went off on their own account to get provisions, and they knew very well where to find them. There were none at Manassas, but by crossing Bull Run and following the line of the Federal retreat, we soon gathered a store sufficient to last us, while the authorities of the quartermaster's department were finding out how to transport the few sheet-iron frying-pans which, with an unnecessary tent here and there, were literally the only things there were to be transported at all. Food, which was the only really necessary thing just then, lay ahead of us and nowhere else. All the ammunition we had we could and did move with the wagons at hand.

To return to the temper of the troops and people. Did the Southerners really think themselves a match for ten times their own numbers? I know the reader wants to ask this question, because almost everybody I talk to on the subject asks it in one shape or another. In answer let me say, I think a few of the more enthusiastic women, cherishing a blind faith in the righteousness of their cause, and believing, in spite of historical precedent, that wars always end with strict regard to the laws of poetic justice, did think something of the sort; and I am certain that all the stump speakers of the kind I have hitherto described held a like faith most devoutly. But with these exceptions I never saw any Southerner who hoped for any but well-fought-for success. It was not a question of success or defeat with them at all. They thought they saw their duty plainly, and they did it without regard to the consequences. Their whole hearts were in the cause, and as they were human beings they naturally learned to expect the result for which they were laboring and fighting and suffering; but they based no hopes upon any such fancy as that the Virginian soldier was the military equivalent of ten or of two Pennsylvanians armed as well as he. On the contrary, they busily counted the chances and weighed the probabilities on both sides from the first. They claimed an advantage in the fact that their young men were more universally accustomed to field sports and the use of arms than were those of the North. They thought too, that, fighting on their own soil, in an essentially defensive struggle, they would have some

advantage, as they certainly did. They thought they might
in the end tire their enemy out, and they hoped from the
first for relief through foreign intervention in some shape.
These were the grounds of their hopes; but had there been
no hope for them at all, I verily believe they would have
fought all the same. Certainly they had small reason to
hope for success after the campaign of 1863, but they fought
on nevertheless, until they could fight no more. Let the
reader remember that as the Southerners understood the
case, they could not, without a complete sacrifice of honor,
do anything else than fight on until utterly crushed, and
he will then be prepared to understand how small a figure
the question of success or failure cut in determining their
course.

The unanimity of the people was simply marvelous. So
long as the question of secession was under discussion, opinions were both various and violent. The moment secession
was finally determined upon, a revolution was wrought.
There was no longer anything to discuss, and so discussion
ceased. Men got ready for war, and delicate women with
equal spirit sent them off with smiling faces. The man who
tarried at home for never so brief a time, after the call
to arms had been given, found it necessary to explain himself to every woman of his acquaintance, and no explanation was sufficient to shield him from the social ostracism
consequent upon any long-tarrying. Throughout the war it
was the same, and when the war ended the men who lived
to return were greeted with sad faces by those who had
cheerfully and even joyously sent them forth to the battle.

Under these circumstances, the reader will readily understand, the first call for troops took nearly all the men of
Virginia away from their homes. Even the boys in the
colleges and schools enlisted, and these establishments were
forced to suspend for want of students. In one college the

president organized the students, and making himself their commander, led them directly from the class-room to the field. So strong and all-embracing was the thought that every man owed it to the community to become a soldier, that even clergymen went into the army by the score, and large districts of country were left too without a physician, until the people could secure, by means of a memorial, the unanimous vote of the company to which some favorite physician belonged, declaring it to be his patriotic duty to remain at home. Without such an instruction from his comrades no physician would consent to withdraw, and even with it very many of them preferred to serve in the ranks.

These were the men of whom the Confederate army was for the first year or two chiefly composed. After that the conscription brought in a good deal of material which was worse than useless. There were some excellent soldiers who came into the army as conscripts, but they were exceptions to the rule. For the most part the men whose bodies were thus lugged in by force had no spirits to bring with them. They had already lived a long time under all the contumely which a reputation for confessed cowardice could bring upon them. The verdict of their neighbors was already pronounced, and they could not possibly change it now by good conduct. They brought discontent with them into the camp, and were sullenly worthless as soldiers throughout. They were a leaven of demoralization which the army would have been better without. But they were comparatively few in number, and as the character of the army was crystallized long before these men came into it at all, they had little influence in determining the conduct of the whole. If they added nothing to our strength, they could do little to weaken us, and in any estimate of the character of the Confederate army they hardly count at all. The men who early in the war struggled for a place in the front rank,

whenever there was chance of a fight, and thought themselves unlucky if they failed to get it, are the men who gave
character afterwards to the well-organized and well-disciplined army which so long contested the ground before
Richmond. They did become soldiers after a while, well
regulated and thoroughly effective. The process of disci-
plining them took away none of their personal spirit or
their personal interest in the war, but it taught them the
value of unquestioning obedience, and the virtue there was
in yielding it. I remember very well the extreme coolness
with which, in one of the valley skirmishes, a few days before the first battle of Bull Run, a gentleman private in my
own company rode out of the ranks for the purpose of sug-
gesting to J. E. B. Stuart the propriety of charging a gun
which was shelling us, and which seemed nearer to us than
to its supporting infantry. I heard another gentleman without rank, who had brought a dispatch to Stonewall Jackson,
request that officer to ''cut the answer short,'' on the ground
that his horse was a little lame and he feared his inability
to deliver it as promptly as was desirable. These men and
their comrades lost none of this personal solicitude for the
proper conduct of the war, in process of becoming soldiers,
but they learned not to question or advise, when their duty
was to listen and obey. Their very errors, as General Stuart
once said in my hearing, proved them the best of material
out of which to make soldiers. ''They are pretty good officers
now,'' he said, ''and after a while they will make excellent
soldiers too. They only need *reducing to the ranks.*''

This personal interest in the war, which in their undisciplined beginning led them into indiscreet meddling with
details of policy belonging to their superiors, served to sustain them when as disciplined soldiers they were called
upon to bear a degree of hardship of which they had never
dreamed. They learned to trust the management of affairs

to the officers, asking no questions, but finding their own greatest usefulness in cheerful and ready obedience. The wish to help, which made them unsoldierly at first, served to make them especially good soldiers when it was duly tempered with discipline and directed by experience. The result was that even in the darkest days of the struggle, when these soldiers knew they were losing everything but their honor, when desperation led them to think of a thousand expedients and to see every blunder that was made, they waited patiently for the word of command, and obeyed it with alacrity and cheerfulness when it came, however absurd it might seem. I remember an incident which will serve to illustrate this. The Federal forces one day captured an important fort on the north side of James River, which had been left almost unguarded, through the blundering of the officer charged with its defense. It must be retaken, or the entire line in that place must be abandoned, and a new one built, at great risk of losing Richmond. Two bodies of infantry were ordered to charge it on different sides, while the command to which I was then attached should shell it vigorously with mortars. In order that the attack might be simultaneously made on the two sides, a specific time was set for it, but for some unexplained reason there was a misunderstanding between the two commanders. The one on the farther side began the attack twenty minutes too soon. Every man of the other body, which lay there by our still silent mortars, knew perfectly well that the attack had begun, and that they ought to strike then if at all. They knew that, without their aid and that of the mortars, their friends would be repulsed, and that a like result would follow their own assault when it should be made, twenty minutes later. They remained as they were, however, hearing the rattle of the musketry and listening with calm faces to the exulting cheers of the victorious enemy. Then came their own time, and knowing perfectly well that their assault was now a useless waste of life, they obeyed the order as it had been delivered to them, and knocked at the very gates of that fortress for an hour. These men, in 1861, would have clamored for immediate attack as the only hope of accomplishing anything, and had their commander insisted, in such a case, upon obeying orders, they would in all probability have charged without him. In 1864, having become soldiers, they obeyed orders even at cost of failure. They had reduced themselves to the ranks—that was all.

CHAPTER 4

THE TEMPER OF THE WOMEN

——————◀●▶——————

URING the latter part of the year in which the war
between the States came to an end, a Southern comic
writer, in a letter addressed to Artemus Ward,
summed up the political outlook in one sentence, reading
somewhat as follows: "You may reconstruct the men, with
your laws and things, but how are you going to reconstruct
the women? *Whoop-ee!*" Now this unauthorized but certainly very expressive interjection had a deal of truth at
its back, and I am very sure that I have never yet known
a thoroughly "reconstructed" woman. The reason, of
course, is not far to seek. The women of the South could
hardly have been more desperately in earnest than their
husbands and brothers and sons were, in the prosecution
of the war, but with their woman-natures they gave themselves wholly to the cause, and having loved it heartily
when it gave promise of a sturdy life, they almost worship
it now that they have strewn its bier with funeral flowers.
To doubt its righteousness, or to falter in their loyalty to
it while it lived, would have been treason and infidelity;
to do the like now that it is dead would be to them little
less than sacrilege.

I wish I could adequately tell my reader of the part those women played in the war. If I could make these pages show the half of their nobleness; if I could describe the sufferings they endured, and tell of their cheerfulness under it all; if the reader might guess the utter unselfishness with which they laid themselves and the things they held nearest their hearts upon the altar of the only country they knew as their own, the rare heroism with which they played their sorrowful part in a drama which was to them a long tragedy; if my pages could be made to show the half of these things, all womankind, I am sure, would tenderly cherish the record, and nobody would wonder again at the tenacity with which the women of the South still hold their allegiance to the lost cause.

Theirs was a peculiarly hard lot. The real sorrows of war, like those of drunkenness, always fall most heavily upon women. They may not bear arms. They may not even share the triumphs which compensate their brethren for toil and suffering and danger. They must sit still and endure. The poverty which war brings to them wears no cheerful face, but sits down with them to empty tables and pinches them sorely in solitude.

After the victory, the men who have won it throw up their hats in a glad huzza, while their wives and daughters await in sorest agony of suspense the news which may bring hopeless desolation to their hearts. To them the victory may mean the loss of those for whom they lived and in whom they hoped, while to those who have fought the battle it brings only gladness. And all this was true of Southern women almost without exception. The fact that all the men capable of bearing arms went into the army, and stayed there, gave to every woman in the South a personal interest not only in the general result of each battle, but in the list of killed and wounded as well. Poverty, too, and privation of the sorest kind, was the common lot, while the absence of the men laid many heavy burdens of work and responsibility upon shoulders unused to either. But they bore it all, not cheerfully only, but gladly. They believed it to be the duty of every able-bodied man to serve in the army, and they eagerly sent the men of their own homes to the field, frowning undisguisedly upon every laggard until there were no laggards left. And their spirit knew no change as the war went on. Their idea of men's duty comprehended nothing less than persistence as long as a shot could be fired. When they saw that the end was not to be victory, but defeat, that fact made no change whatever in their view of the duty to be done. Still less did their own privations and labors and sufferings tend to dampen their ardor. On the contrary, the more heavily the war bore upon themselves, the more persistently did they demand that it should be fought out to the end. When they lost a husband, a son, or a brother, they held the loss only an additional reason for faithful adherence to the cause. Having made such a sacrifice to that which was almost a religion to them, they had, if possible, less thought than ever of proving unfaithful to it.

I put these general statements first, so that the reader who shall be interested in such anecdotes as I shall have to tell may not be misled thereby into the thought that these good women were implacable or vindictive, when they were only devoted to a cause which in their eyes represented the sum of all righteousness.

I remember a conversation between two of them—one a young wife whose husband was in the army, and the other an elderly lady, with no husband or son, but with many friends and near relatives in marching regiments. The younger lady remarked—

"I'm sure I do not hate our enemies. I earnestly hope

their souls may go to heaven, but I would like to blow all their mortal bodies away, as fast as they come upon our soil.''

''Why, you shock me, my dear,'' replied the other; ''I don't see why you want the Yankees to go to heaven! I hope to get there myself some day, and I'm sure I shouldn't want to go if I thought I should find any of them there.''

This old lady was convinced from the first that the South would fail, and she based this belief upon the fact that we had permitted Yankees to build railroads through the Southern States. ''I tell you,'' she would say, ''that's what they built the railroads for. They knew the war was coming, and they got ready for it. The railroads will whip us, you may depend. What else were they made for? We got on well enough without them, and we oughtn't to have let anybody build them.'' And no amount of reasoning would serve to shake her conviction that the people of the North had built all our railroads with treacherous intent, though the stock of the only road she had ever seen was held very largely by the people along its line, many of whom were her own friends.

She always insisted, too, that the Northern troops came South and made war for the sole purpose of taking possession of our lands and Negroes, and she was astonished almost out of her wits when she learned that the Negroes were free. She had supposed that they were simply to change masters, and even then she lived for months in daily anticipation of the coming of ''the new land owners,'' who were waiting, she supposed, for assignments of plantations to be made to them by military authority.

''They'll quarrel about the division, maybe,'' she said one day, ''and then there'll be a chance for us to whip them again, I hope.'' The last time I saw her, she had not yet become convinced that title-deeds were still to be respected.

A young girl, ordinarily of a very gentle disposition, astonished a Federal colonel one day by an outburst of temper which served at least to show the earnestness of her purpose to uphold her side of the argument. She lived in a part of the country then for the first time held by the Federal army, and a colonel, with some members of his staff, made her family the unwilling recipients of a call one morning. Seeing the piano open, the colonel asked the young lady to play, but she declined. He then went to the instrument himself, but he had hardly begun to play when the damsel, raising the piano top, severed nearly all the strings with a hatchet, saying to the astonished performer, as she did so—

"That's my piano, and it shall not give you a minute's pleasure." The colonel bowed, apologized, and replied—

"If all your people are as ready as you to make costly sacrifices, we might as well go home."

And most of them were ready and willing to make similar sacrifices. One lady of my acquaintance knocked in the heads of a dozen casks of choice wine rather than allow some Federal officers to sip as many glasses of it. Another destroyed her own library, which was very precious to her, when that seemed the only way in which she could prevent the staff of a general officer, camped near her, from enjoying a few hours' reading in her parlor every morning.

In New Orleans, soon after the war, I saw in a drawing-room, one day, an elaborately framed letter, of which, the curtains being drawn, I could read only the signature, which to my astonishment was that of General Butler.

"What is that?" I asked of the young gentlewoman I was visiting.

"Oh, that's my diploma, my certificate of good behavior, from General Butler;" and taking it down from the wall, she permitted me to read it, telling me at the same time its history. It seems that the young lady had been very active in aiding captured Confederates to escape from New Orleans, and for this and other similar offenses she was arrested several times. A gentleman who knew General Butler personally had interested himself in behalf of her and some of her friends, and upon making an appeal for their discharge received this personal note from the commanding general, in which he declared his willingness to discharge all the others, "But that black-eyed Miss B.," he wrote, "seems to me an incorrigible little devil whom even prison fare won't tame." The young lady had framed the note, and she cherishes it yet, doubtless.

There is a story told of General Forrest, which will serve to show his opinion of the pluck and devotion of the Southern women. He was drawing his men up in line of battle one day, and it was evident that a sharp encounter was about to take place. Some ladies ran from a house, which happened to stand just in front of his line, and asked him anxiously—

"What shall we do, general, what shall we do?"

Strong in his faith that they only wished to help in some way, he replied,—

"I really don't see that you can do much, except to stand on stumps, wave your bonnets, and shout 'Hurrah, boys!'"

In Richmond, when the hospitals were filled with wounded men brought in from the seven days' fighting with McClellan, and the surgeons found it impossible to dress half the wounds, a band was formed, consisting of nearly all the married women of the city, who took upon themselves the duty of going to the hospitals and dressing wounds from morning till night; and they persisted in their painful duty until every man was cared for, saving hundreds of lives, as the surgeons unanimously testified. When nitre was found to be growing scarce, and the supply of gunpowder was consequently about to give out, women all over the land dug up the earth in their smoke-houses and tobacco barns, and with their own hands faithfully extracted the desired salt, for use in the government laboratories.

Many of them denied themselves not only delicacies, but substantial food also, when by enduring semi-starvation they could add to the stock of food at the command of the subsistence officers. I myself knew more than one houseful of women, who, from the moment that food began to grow scarce, refused to eat meat or drink coffee, living thenceforth only upon vegetables of a speedily perishable sort, in order that they might leave the more for the soldiers in the field. When a friend remonstrated with one of them, on the ground that her health, already frail, was breaking down utterly for want of proper diet, she replied, in a quiet, determined way, ''I know that very well; but it is little that I can do, and I must do that little at any cost. My health and my life are worth less than those of my brothers, and if they give theirs to the cause, why should not I do the same? I would starve to death cheerfully if I could feed one soldier more by doing so, but the things I eat can't be sent to camp. I think it a sin to eat anything that can be used for rations.'' And she meant what she said, too, as a little mound in the church-yard testifies.

Every Confederate remembers gratefully the reception given him when he went into any house where these women were. Whoever he might be, and whatever his plight, if he wore the gray, he was received, not as a beggar or tramp, not even as a stranger, but as a son of the house, for whom it held nothing too good, and whose comfort was the one care of all its inmates, even though their own must be sacrificed in securing it. When the hospitals were crowded, the people earnestly besought permission to take the men to their houses and to care for them there, and for many months almost every house within a hundred miles of Richmond held one or more wounded men as especially honored guests.

"God bless these Virginia women!" said a general officer from one of the cotton States, one day, "they're worth a regiment apiece;" and he spoke the thought of the army, except that their blessing covered the whole country as well as Virginia.

The ingenuity with which these good ladies discovered or manufactured onerous duties for themselves was surprising, and having discovered or imagined some new duty they straightway proceeded to do it at any cost. An excellent Richmond dame was talking with a soldier friend, when he carelessly remarked that there was nothing which so greatly helped to keep up a contented and cheerful spirit among the men as the receipt of letters from their woman friends. Catching at the suggestion as a revelation of duty, she asked, "And cheerfulness makes better soldiers of the men, does it not?" Receiving yes for an answer, the frail little woman, already overburdened with cares of an unusual sort, sat down and made out a list of all the men with whom she was acquainted even in the smallest possible way, and from that day until the end of the war she wrote one letter a week to each, a task which, as her acquaintance was large, taxed her time and strength very severely. Not content with this, she wrote on the subject in the newspapers, earnestly urging a like course upon her sisters, many of whom adopted the suggestion at once, much to the delight of the soldiers, who little dreamed that the kindly, cheerful, friendly letters which every mail brought into camp, were a part of woman's self-appointed work for the success of the common cause. From the beginning to the end of the war it was the same. No cry of pain escaped woman's lips at the parting which sent the men into camp;

no word of despondency was spoken when hope seemed most surely dead; no complaint from the women ever reminded their soldier husbands and sons and brothers that there was hardship and privation and terror at home. They bore all with brave hearts and cheerful faces, and even when they mourned the death of their most tenderly loved ones, they comforted themselves with the thought that they buried only heroic dust.

"It is the death I would have chosen for him," wrote the widow of a friend whose loss I had announced to her. "I loved him for his manliness, and now that he has shown that manliness by dying as a hero dies, I mourn, but am not broken-hearted. I know that a brave man awaits me whither I am going."

They carried their efforts to cheer and help the troops into every act of their lives. When they could, they visited camp. Along the lines of march they came out with water or coffee or tea—the best they had, whatever it might be— with flowers, or garlands of green when their flowers were gone. A bevy of girls stood under a sharp fire from the enemy's lines at Petersburg one day, while they sang Bayard Taylor's Song of the Camp, responding to an encore with the stanza:—

> Ah! soldiers, to your honored rest,
>   Your truth and valor bearing,
> The bravest are the tenderest,
>   The loving are the daring!

Indeed, the coolness of women under fire was always a matter of surprise to me. A young girl, not more than sixteen years of age, acted as guide to a scouting party during the early years of the war, and when we urged her to go back after the enemy had opened a vigorous fire upon us, she declined, on the plea that she believed we were "going to charge those fellows," and she "wanted to see the fun." At Petersburg women did their shopping and went about their duties under a most uncomfortable bombardment, without evincing the slightest fear or showing any nervousness whatever.

But if the cheerfulness of the women during the war was remarkable, what shall we say of the way in which they met its final failure and the poverty that came with it? The end of the war completed the ruin which its progress had wrought. Women who had always lived in luxury, and whose labors and sufferings during the war were lightened by the consciousness that in suffering and laboring they were doing their part toward the accomplishment of the end upon which all hearts were set, were now compelled to face not temporary but permanent poverty, and to endure, without a motive or a sustaining purpose, still sorer privations than any they had known in the past. The country was exhausted, and nobody could foresee any future but one of abject wretchedness. It was seed-time, but the suddenly freed Negroes had not yet learned that freedom meant aught else than idleness, and the spring was gone before anything like a reorganization of the labor system could be effected. The men might emigrate when they should get home, but the case of the women was a very sorry one indeed. They kept their spirits up through it all, however, and improvised a new social system in which absolute poverty, cheerfully borne, was the badge of respectability. Everybody was poor except the speculators who had fattened upon the necessities of the women and children, and so poverty was essential to anything like good repute. The return of the soldiers made some sort of social festivity necessary, and "starvation parties" were given, at which it was understood that the givers were wholly unable to set out refreshments of any kind.

In the matter of dress, too, the general poverty was recognized, and every one went clad in whatever he or she happened to have. The want of means became a jest, and nobody mourned over it; while all were laboring to repair their wasted fortunes as they best could. And all this was due solely to the unconquerable cheerfulness of the Southern women. The men came home moody, worn out, discouraged, and but for the influence of woman's cheerfulness, the Southern States might have fallen into a lethargy from which they could not have recovered for generations.

Such prosperity as they have since achieved is largely due to the courage and spirit of their noble women.

CHAPTER 5

OF THE TIME WHEN MONEY WAS

"EASY"

———◆●▶———

IT SEEMS a remarkable fact that during the late Congressional travail with the currency question, no one of the people in or out of Congress, who were concerned lest there should not be enough money in the country to "move the crops," ever took upon himself the pleasing task of rehearsing the late Confederacy's financial story, for the purpose of showing by example how simple and easy a thing it is to create wealth out of nothing by magic revolutions of the printing-press, and to make rich, by act of Congress, everybody not too lazy to gather free dollars into a pile. The story has all the flavor of the Princess Scheherezade's romances, with the additional merit of being historically true. For once a whole people was rich. Money was "easy" enough to satisfy everybody, and everybody had it in unstinted measure. This money was not, it is true, of a quality to please the believers in a gold or other arbitrary standard of value, but that is a matter of little consequence, now that senators and representatives of high repute have shown that the best currency possible is that which exists only by the will of the government, and the volume of which is regulated by the cravings of the people alone. That so apt an illustration of the financial views of the majority in Congress should have been wholly neglected, during the discussions, seems therefore unaccountable.

The financial system adopted by the Confederate government was singularly simple and free from technicalities. It consisted chiefly in the issue of treasury notes enough to meet all the expenses of the government, and in the present advanced state of the art of printing there was but one difficulty incident to this process; namely, the impossibility of having the notes signed in the Treasury Department, as fast as they were needed. There happened, however, to be several thousand young ladies in Richmond willing to accept light and remunerative employment at their homes, and as it was really a matter of small moment whose name the notes bore, they were given out in sheets to these young ladies, who signed and returned them for a consideration. I shall not undertake to guess how many Confederate treasury notes were issued. Indeed I am credibly informed by a gentleman who was high in office in the Treasury Department, that even the secretary himself did not certainly know. The acts of Congress authorizing issues of currency were the hastily formulated thought of a not very wise body of men, and my informant tells me they were frequently susceptible of widely different construction by different officials. However that may be, it was clearly out of the power of the government ever to redeem the notes, and whatever may have been the state of affairs within the treasury, nobody outside its precincts ever cared to muddle his head in an attempt to get at exact figures.

We knew only that money was astonishingly abundant. Provisions fell short sometimes, and the supply of clothing was not always as large as we should have liked, but nobody found it difficult to get money enough. It was to be had almost for the asking. And to some extent the abundance of the currency really seemed to atone for its extreme badness. Going the rounds of the pickets on the coast of South Carolina, one day, in 1863, I heard a conversation between a Confederate and a Union soldier, stationed on opposite sides of a little inlet, in the course of which this point was brought out.

UNION SOLDIER. Aren't times rather hard over there, Johnny?

CONFEDERATE SOLDIER. Not at all. We've all the necessaries of life.

U. S. Yes; but how about luxuries? You never see any coffee nowadays, do you?

C. S. Plenty of it.

U. S. Isn't it pretty high?

C. S. Forty dollars a pound, that's all.

U. S. Whew! Don't you call that high?

C. S. (after reflecting). Well, perhaps it is a trifle uppish, but then you never saw money so plentiful as it is with us. We hardly know what to do with it, and don't mind paying high prices for things we want.

And that was the universal feeling. Money was so easily got, and its value was so utterly uncertain, that we were never able to determine what was a fair price for anything. We fell into the habit of paying whatever was asked, knowing that to-morrow we should have to pay more. Speculation became the easiest and surest thing imaginable. The speculator saw no risks of loss. Every article of merchandise rose in value every day, and to buy anything this week and sell it next was to make an enormous profit quite as a matter of course. So uncertain were prices, or rather so constantly did they tend upward, that when a cargo of cadet gray cloths was brought into Charleston once, an officer in my battery,

attending the sale, was able to secure enough of the cloth
to make two suits of clothes, without any expense whatever,
merely by speculating upon an immediate advance. He became the purchaser, at auction, of a case of the goods, and
had no difficulty, as soon as the sale was over, in finding a
merchant who was glad to take his bargain off his hands,
giving him the cloth he wanted as a premium. The officer
could not possibly have paid for the case of goods, but there
was nothing surer than that he could sell again at an advance the moment the auctioneer's hammer fell on the last
lot of cloths.

Naturally enough, speculation soon fell into very bad
repute, and the epithet "speculator" came to be considered
the most opprobrious in the whole vocabulary of invective.
The feeling was universal that the speculators were fatten-
ing upon the necessities of the country and the sufferings of
the people. Nearly all mercantile business was regarded at
least with suspicion, and much of it fell into the hands of
people with no reputations to lose, a fact which certainly
did not tend to relieve the community in the matter of high
prices.

The prices which obtained were almost fabulous, and
singularly enough there seemed to be no sort of ratio existing between the values of different articles. I bought coffee
at forty dollars and tea at thirty dollars a pound on the
same day.

My dinner at a hotel cost me twenty dollars, while five
dollars gained me a seat in the dress circle of the theatre.
I paid one dollar the next morning for a copy of the *Examiner,* but I might have got the *Whig, Dispatch, Enquirer,*
or *Sentinel,* for half that sum. For some wretched tallow
candles I paid ten dollars a pound. The utter absence of proportion between these several prices is apparent, and I know
of no way of explaining it except upon the theory that the

unstable character of the money had superinduced a reckless disregard of all value on the part of both buyers and sellers. A facetious friend used to say prices were so high that nobody could see them, and that they "got mixed for want of supervision." He held, however, that the difference between the old and the new order of things was a trifling one. "Before the war," he said, "I went to market with the money in my pocket, and brought back my purchases in a basket; now I take the money in the basket, and bring the things home in my pocket."

As I was returning to my home after the surrender at Appomattox Court House, a party of us stopped at the residence of a planter for supper, and as the country was full of marauders and horse thieves, deserters from both armies, bent upon indiscriminate plunder, our host set a little black boy to watch our horses while we ate, with instructions to give the alarm if anybody should approach. After supper we dealt liberally with little Sam. Silver and gold we had none, of course, but Confederate money was ours in great abundance, and we bestowed the crisp notes upon the guardian of our horses, to the extent of several hundreds of dollars. A richer person than that little Negro I have never seen. Money, even at par, never carried more of happiness with it than did those promises of a dead government to pay. We frankly told Sam that he could buy nothing with the notes, but the information brought no sadness to his simple heart.

"I don' want to buy nothin', master," he replied. "I's gwine to keep dis al*ways*."

I fancy his regard for the worthless paper, merely because it was called money, was closely akin to the feeling which had made it circulate among better-informed people than he. Everybody knew, long before the surrender, that these notes never could be redeemed. There was little reason to hope, during the last two years of the war, that the "ratification of a treaty of peace between the Confederate States and the United States," on which the payment was conditioned, would ever come. We knew the paper was worthless, and yet it continued to circulate. It professed to be money, and on the strength of that profession people continued to take it in payment for goods. The amount of it for which the owner of any article would part with his possession was always uncertain. Prices were regulated largely by accident, and were therefore wholly incongruous.

But the disproportion between the prices of different articles was not greater than that between the cost of goods imported through the blockade and their selling price. The usual custom of blockade-running firms was to build or buy a steamer in Europe, bring it to Nassau in ballast, and load it there with assorted merchandise. Selling this cargo in Charleston or Wilmington for Confederate money, they would buy cotton with which to reload the ship for her outward voyage. The owner of many of these ships once told me that if a vessel which had brought in one cargo were lost with a load of cotton on her outward voyage, the owner would lose nothing, the profits on the merchandise being fully equal to the entire value of ship and cotton. If he could get one cargo of merchandise in, and one of cotton out, the loss of the ship with a second cargo of merchandise would still leave him a clear profit of more than a hundred per cent upon his investment. And this was due solely to the abnormal state of prices in the country, and not at all to the management of the blockade-runners. They sold their cargoes at auction, and bought cotton in the open market.

Their merchandise brought fabulous prices, while cotton, for want of a market, remained disproportionately low. That the merchants engaged in this trade were in no way the authors of the state of prices may be seen from two facts. First, if I am correctly informed, they uniformly gave the government an opportunity to take such articles as it had need of, and especially all the quinine imported, at the price fixed in Richmond, without regard to the fact that speculators would pay greatly more for the goods. In one case within my own knowledge a heavy invoice of quinine was sold to the government for eleven hundred dollars an ounce, when a speculator stood ready to take it at double that price. Secondly, the cargo sales were peremptory, and speculators sometimes combined and bought a cargo considerably below the market price, by appearing at the sale in such numbers as to exclude all other bidders. In one case, I remember, the general commanding at Charleston annulled a cargo sale on this account, and sent some of the speculators to jail for the purpose of giving other people an opportunity to purchase needed goods at prices very much higher than those forced upon the sellers by the combination at the first sale.

In the winter of 1863–64 Congress became aware of the fact that prices were higher than they should be under a sound currency. If Congress suspected this at any earlier date, there is nothing in the proceedings of that body to indicate it. Now, however, the newspapers were calling attention to an uncommonly ugly phase of the matter, and reminding Congress that what the government bought with a currency depreciated to less than one per cent of its face, the government must some day pay for in gold at par. The lawgivers took the alarm and sat themselves down to devise a remedy for the evil condition of affairs. With that infantile simplicity which characterized nearly all the doings and quite all the financial legislation of the Richmond Congress, it was decided that the very best way to enhance the value of the currency was to depreciate it still further by a declaratory statute, and then to issue a good deal more of it.

The act set a day, after which the currency already in circulation should be worth only two thirds of its face, at which rate it was made convertible into notes of the new issue, which some, at least, of the members of Congress were innocent enough to believe would be worth very nearly their par value. This measure was intended, of course, to compel the funding of the currency, and it had that effect to some extent, without doubt. Much of the old currency remained in circulation, however, even after the new notes were issued. For a time people calculated the discount, in passing and receiving the old paper, but as the new notes showed an undiminished tendency to still further depreciation, there were people, not a few, who spared themselves the trouble of making the distinction.

I am sometimes asked at what time prices attained their highest point in the Confederacy, and I find that memory fails to answer the question satisfactorily. They were about as high as they could be in the fall of 1863, and I should be disposed to fix upon that as the time when the climax was reached, but for my consciousness that the law of constant appreciation was a fixed one throughout the war. The financial condition got steadily worse to the end. I believe the highest price, relatively, I ever saw paid, was for a pair of boots. A cavalry officer, entering a little country store, found there one pair of boots which fitted him. He inquired the price. "Two hundred dollars," said the merchant. A five hundred dollar bill was offered, but the merchant, having no smaller bills, could not change it. "Never mind," said the cavalier, "I'll take the boots anyhow. Keep the change; I never let a little matter of three hundred dollars stand in the way of a trade."

That was on the day before Lee's surrender, but it would not have been an impossible occurrence at any time during the preceding year. The money was of so little value that we parted with it gladly whenever it would purchase anything at all desirable. I cheerfully paid five dollars for a little salt, at Petersburg, in August, 1864, and being thirsty drank my last two dollars in a half-pint of cider.

The government's course in levying a tax in kind, as the only possible way of making the taxation amount to anything, led speedily to the adoption of a similar plan, as far as possible, by the people. A physician would order from his planter friend ten or twenty visits' worth of corn, and the transaction was a perfectly intelligible one to both. The visits would be counted at ante-war rates, and the corn estimated by the same standard. In the early spring of 1865 I wanted a horse, and a friend having one to spare, I sent for the animal, offering to pay whatever the owner should ask for it. He could not fix a price, having literally no standard of value to which he could appeal, but he sent me the horse, writing, in reply to my note—

"Take the horse, and when the war shall be over, if we are both alive and you are able, give me as good a one in return. Don't send any note or due-bill. It might complicate matters if either should die."

A few months later, I paid my debt by returning the very horse I had bought. I give this incident merely to show how utterly without financial compass or rudder we were.

How did people manage to live during such a time? I am often asked; and as I look back at the history of those years, I can hardly persuade myself that the problem was solved at all. A large part of the people, however, was in the army, and drew rations from the government. During the early years of the war, officers were not given rations, but were allowed to buy provisions from the commissaries at government prices. Subsequently, however, when provisions became so scarce that it was necessary to limit the amount consumed by officers as well as that eaten by the men, the purchase system was abolished, and the whole army was fed upon daily rations. The country people raised upon their plantations all the necessaries of life, and were generally allowed to keep enough of them to live on, the remainder being taken by the subsistence officers for army use. The problem of a salt supply, on which depended the production of meat, was solved in part by the establishment of small salt factories along the coast, and in part by Governor Letcher's vigorous management of the works in south-western Virginia, and his wise distribution of the product along the various lines of railroad.

In the cities, living was not by any means so easy as in the country. Business was paralyzed, and abundant as money was, it seems almost incredible that city people got enough of it to live on. Very many of them were employed, however, in various capacities, in the arsenals, departments, bureaus, etc., and these were allowed to buy rations at fixed rates, after the post-office clerks in Richmond had brought matters to a crisis by resigning their clerkships to go into the army, because they could not support life on their salaries of nine thousand dollars a year. For the rest, if people had anything to sell, they got enormous prices for it, and could live a while on the proceeds. Above all, a kindly, helpful spirit was developed by the common suffering, and this, without doubt, kept many thousands of people from starvation. Those who had anything shared it freely with those who had nothing. There was no selfish looking for-ward, and no hoarding for the time to come. During those terrible last years, the future had nothing of pleasantness in its face, and people learned not to think of it at all. To get through to-day was the only care. Nobody formed any plans or laid by any money for to-morrow or next week or next year, and indeed to most of us there really seemed to be no future. I remember the start it gave me when a clergyman, visiting camp, asked a number of us whether our long stay in defensive works did not afford us an excellent opportunity to study with a view to our professional life after the war. We were not used to think of ourselves as possible survivors of a struggle which was every day perceptibly thinning our ranks. The coming of ultimate failure we saw clearly enough, but the future beyond was a blank. The subject was naturally not a pleasant one, and by common consent it was always avoided in conversation, until at last we learned to avoid it in thought as well. We waited gloomily for the end, but did not care particularly to speculate upon the question when and how the end was to come. There was a vague longing for rest, which found vent now and then in wild newspaper stories of signs and omens portending the close of the war, but beyond this the matter was hardly ever discussed. We had early forbidden ourselves to think of any end to the struggle except a successful one, and that being now an impossibility, we avoided the subject altogether. The newspaper stories to which reference is made above were of the wildest and absurdest sort. One Richmond paper issued an extra, in which it was gravely stated that there was a spring near Fredericksburg which had ceased to flow thirty days before the surrender of the British at Yorktown, thirty days before the termination of the war of 1812, and thirty days before the Mexican war ended; and that "this singularly prophetic fountain has now again ceased to pour forth its waters." At another time a hen near Lynchburg laid an egg, the newspapers said, on which were traced, in occult letters, the words, "peace in ninety days."

Will the reader believe that with gold at a hundred and twenty-five for one, or twelve thousand four hundred per cent premium; when every day made the hopelessness of the struggle more apparent; when our last man was in the field;

when the resources of the country were visibly at an end, there were financial theorists who honestly believed that by a mere trick of legislation the currency could be brought back to par? I heard some of these people explain their plan during a two days' stay in Richmond. Gold, they said, is an inconvenient currency always, and nobody wants it, except as a basis. The government has some gold—several millions in fact—and if Congress will only be bold enough to declare the treasury notes redeemable at par in coin, we shall have no further difficulty with our finances. So long as notes are redeemable in gold at the option of the holder, nobody wants them redeemed. Let the government say to the people, We will redeem the currency whenever you wish, and nobody except a few timid and unpatriotic people will care to change their convenient for an inconvenient money. The gold which the government holds will suffice to satisfy these timid ones, and there will be an end of high prices and depreciated currency. The government can then issue as much more currency as circumstances may make necessary, and strong in our confidence in ourselves we shall be the richest people on earth; we shall have *created* the untold wealth which our currency represents.

I am not jesting. This is, as nearly as I can repeat it, the utterance of a member of the Confederate Congress made in my presence in a private parlor. If the reader thinks the man was insane, I beg him to look over the reports of the debates on financial matters which have been held in Washington.

The effects of the extreme depreciation of the currency were sometimes almost ludicrous. One of my friends, a Richmond lady, narrowly escaped very serious trouble in an effort to practice a wise economy. Anything for which the dealers did not ask an outrageously high price seemed wonderfully cheap always, and she, at least, lacked the self-control necessary to abstain from buying largely whenever she found anything the price of which was lower than she had supposed it would be. Going into market one morning with "stimulated ideas of prices," as she phrased it, the consequence of having paid a thousand dollars for a barrel of flour, she was surprised to find nearly everything selling for considerably less than she had expected. Thinking that for some unexplained cause there was a temporary depression in prices, she purchased pretty largely in a good many directions, buying, indeed, several things for which she had almost no use at all, and buying considerably more than she needed of other articles. As she was quitting the market on foot—for it had become disreputable in Richmond to ride in a carriage, and the ladies would not do it on any account —she was tapped on the shoulder by an officer who told her she was under arrest, for buying in market to sell again. As the lady was well known to prominent people she was speedily released, but she thereafter curbed her propensity to buy freely of cheap things. Buying to sell again had been forbidden under severe penalties—an absolutely necessary measure for the protection of the people against the rapacity of the hucksters, who, going early into the markets, would buy literally everything there, and by agreement among themselves double or quadruple the already exorbitant rates. It became necessary also to suppress the gambling-houses in the interest of the half-starved people. At such a time, of course, gambling was a very common vice, and the gamblers made Richmond their head-quarters. It was the custom of the proprietors of these establishments to set costly suppers in their parlors every night, for the purpose of attracting visitors likely to become victims. For these suppers they must have the best of everything without stint, and their lavish rivalry in the poorly stocked markets had the effect of advancing prices to a dangerous point. To suppress the gambling-houses was the sole remedy, and it was only by uncommonly severe measures that the suppression could be accomplished. It was therefore enacted that any one found guilty of keeping a gambling-house should be publicly whipped upon the bare back, and as the infliction of the penalty in one or two instances effectually and permanently broke up the business of gambling, even in the disorganized and demoralized state in which society then was, it may be said with confidence that whipping is the one certain remedy for this evil. Whether it be not, in ordinary cases, worse than the evil which it cures, it is not our business just now to inquire.

The one thing which we were left almost wholly without, during the war, was literature. Nobody thought of importing books through the blockade, to any adequate extent, and the facilities for publishing them, even if we had had authors to write them, were very poor indeed. A Mobile firm reprinted a few of the more popular books of the time, *Les Misérables, Great Expectations,* etc., and I have a pamphlet edition of Owen Meredith's *Tannhäuser,* bound in coarse wall-paper, for which I paid seven dollars, in Charleston. Singularly enough, I bought at the same time a set of Dickens's works, of English make, well printed and bound in black cloth, for four dollars a volume, a discrepancy which I am wholly unable to explain. In looking through a file of the Richmond *Examiner* extending over most of the year 1864, I find but one book of any sort advertised, and the price of that, a duodecimo volume of only 72 pages, was five dollars, the publishers promising to send it by mail, post-paid, on receipt of the price.

Towards the last, as I have already said, resort was had frequently to first principles, and bartering, or "payment in kind," as it was called, became common, especially in those cases in which it was necessary to announce prices in advance. To fix a price for the future in Confederate money when it was daily becoming more and more exaggeratedly worthless, would have been sheer folly; and so educational institutions, country boarding-houses, etc., advertised for patronage at certain prices, payment to be made in provisions at the rates prevailing in September, 1860. In the advertisement of Hampden Sidney College, in the *Examiner* for October 4, 1864, I find it stated that students may get board in private families at about eight dollars a month, payable in this way. The strong contrast between the prices of 1860 and those of 1864 is shown by a statement, in the same advertisement, that the students who may get board at eight dollars a month in provisions, can buy wood at twenty-five dollars a cord and get their washing done for seven dollars and fifty cents a dozen pieces.

This matter of prices was frequently made a subject for jesting in private, but for the most part it was carefully avoided in the newspapers. It was too ominous of evil to be a fit topic of editorial discussion on ordinary occasions. As with the accounts of battles in which our arms were not successful, necessary references to the condition of the finances were crowded into a corner, as far out of sight as possible. The *Examiner,* being a sort of newspaper Ishmael, did now and then bring the subject up, however, and on one occasion it denounced with some fierceness the charges prevailing in the schools; and I quote a passage from Prof. Sidney H. Owens's reply, which is interesting as a summary of the condition of things in the South at that time:—

"The charges made for tuition are about five or six times as high as in 1860. Now, sir, your shoemaker, carpenter, butcher, market man, etc., demand from twenty, to thirty, to forty times as much as in 1860. Will you show me a civilian who is charging only six times the prices charged in 1860, except the teacher only? As to the amassing of fortunes by teachers, spoken of in your article, make your calculations, sir, and you will find that to be almost an absurdity, since they pay from twenty to forty prices for everything used, and are denounced exorbitant and unreasonable in demanding five or six prices for their own labor and skill.''

There were compensations, however. When gold was at twelve thousand per cent premium with us, we had the consolation of knowing that it was in the neighborhood of one hundred above par in New York, and a Richmond paper of September 22, 1864, now before me, fairly chuckles over the high prices prevailing at the North, in a two-line paragraph which says, ''Tar is selling in New York at two dollars a pound. It used to cost eighty cents a barrel.'' That paragraph doubtless made many a five-dollar beefsteak palatable.

CHAPTER 6

THE CHEVALIER OF THE LOST
CAUSE

————◆◆►————

T HE queer people who devote their energies to the collection of autographs have a habit, as everybody whose
name has been three times in print must have discovered, of soliciting from their victim "an autograph *with* a
sentiment," and the unfortunate one is expected, in such
cases, to say something worthy of himself, something especially which shall be eminently characteristic, revealing, in
a single sentence, the whole man, or woman, as the case may
be. How large a proportion of the efforts to do this are
measurably successful, nobody but a collector of the sort
referred to can say; but it seeems probable that the most
characteristic autograph "sentiments" are those which are
written of the writer's own motion and not of malice afore-
thought. I remember seeing a curious collection of these
once, many of which were certainly not unworthy the men
who wrote them. One read, "I. O. U. fifty pounds lost at
play—CHARLES JAMES FOX;" and another was a memoran-
dum of sundry wagers laid, signed by the Right Honorable
Richard Brinsley Sheridan. These, I thought, bore the impress of their authors' character, and it is at the least doubtful whether either of the distinguished gentlemen would

have done half so well in answer to a modest request for a sentiment and a signature.

In the great dining-hall of the Briars, an old-time mansion in the Shenandoah Valley, the residence of Mr. John Esten Cooke, there hangs a portrait of a broad-shouldered cavalier, and beneath is written, in the hand of the cavalier himself,

Yours to count on,
J. E. B. STUART.

an autograph sentiment which seems to me a very perfect one in its way. There was no point in Stuart's character more strongly marked than the one here hinted at. He was "yours to count on" always: your friend if possible, your enemy if you would have it so, but your friend or your enemy "to count on," in any case. A franker, more transparent nature, it is impossible to conceive. What he was he professed to be. That which he thought, he said, and his habit of thinking as much good as he could of those about him served to make his frankness of speech a great friend-winner.

I saw him for the first time when he was a colonel, in command of the little squadron of horsemen known as the first regiment of Virginia cavalry. The company to which I belonged was assigned to this regiment immediately after the evacuation of Harper's Ferry by the Confederates. General Johnston's army was at Winchester, and the Federal force under General Patterson lay around Martinsburg. Stuart, with his three or four hundred men, was encamped at Bunker Hill, about midway between the two, and thirteen miles from support of any kind. He had chosen this position as a convenient one from which to observe the movements of the enemy, and the tireless activity which marked his subsequent career so strongly had already begun. As he afterwards explained, it was his purpose to train and school his men, quite as much as anything else, that prompted the greater part of his madcap expeditions at this time, and if there be virtue in practice as a means of perfection, he was certainly an excellent school-master.

My company arrived at the camp about noon, after a march of three or four days, having traveled twenty miles that morning. Stuart, whom we encountered as we entered the camp, assigned us our position, and ordered our tents pitched. Our captain, who was even worse disciplined than we were, seeing a much more comfortable camping-place than the muddy one assigned to us, and being a comfort-loving gentleman, proceeded to pay out a model camp at a distance of fifty yards from the spot indicated. It was not long before the colonel particularly wished to consult with that captain, and after the consultation the volunteer officer was firmly convinced that all West Point graduates were martinets, with no knowledge whatever of the courtesies due from one gentleman to another.

We were weary after our long journey, and disposed to welcome the prospect of rest which our arrival in the camp held out. But resting, as we soon learned, had small place in our colonel's tactics. We had been in camp perhaps an hour, when an order came directing that the company be divided into three parts, each under command of a lieutenant, and that these report immediately for duty. Reporting, we were directed to scout through the country around Martinsburg, going as near the town as possible, and to give battle to any cavalry force we might meet. Here was a pretty lookout, certainly! Our officers knew not one inch of the country, and might fall into all sorts of traps and ambuscades; and what if we should meet a cavalry force greatly superior to our own? This West Point colonel was rapidly forfeiting our good opinion. Our lieutenants were brave fellows, however, and they led us boldly if ignorantly, almost up to the very gates of the town occupied by the enemy. We saw some cavalry but met none, their orders not being so peremptorily belligerent, perhaps, as ours were; wherefore they gave us no chance to fight them. The next morning our unreasonable colonel again ordered us to mount, in spite of the fact that there were companies in the camp which had done nothing at all the day before. This time he led us himself, taking pains to get us as nearly as possible surrounded by infantry, and then laughingly telling us that our chance for getting out of the difficulty, except by cutting our way through, was an exceedingly small one. I think we began about this time to suspect that we were learning something, and that this reckless colonel was trying to teach us. But that he was a hare-brained fellow, lacking the caution belonging to a commander, we were unanimously agreed. He led us out of the place at a rapid gait, before the one gap in the enemy's lines could be closed, and then jauntily led us into one or two other traps, before taking us back to camp.

But it was not until General Patterson began his feint against Winchester that our colonel had full opportunity to give us his field lectures. When the advance began, and our pickets were driven in, the most natural thing to do, in our view of the situation, was to fall back upon our infantry supports at Winchester, and I remember hearing various expressions of doubt as to the colonel's sanity when, instead of falling back, he marched his handful of men right up to the advancing lines, and ordered us to dismount. The Federal skirmish line was coming toward us at a double-quick, and we were set going toward it at a like rate of speed, leaving our horses hundreds of yards to the rear. We could see that the skirmishers alone outnumbered us three or four times, and it really seemed that our colonel meant to sacrifice his command deliberately. He waited until the infantry was within about two hundred yards of us, we being in the edge of a little grove, and they on the other side of an open field. Then Stuart cried out, ''Backwards—march! steady, men— keep your faces to the enemy!'' and we marched in that way through the timber, delivering our shot-gun fire slowly as we fell back toward our horses. Then mounting, with the skirmishers almost upon us, we retreated, not hurriedly, but at a slow trot, which the colonel would on no account permit us to change into a gallop. Taking us out into the main road he halted us in column, with our backs to the enemy.

''Attention!'' he cried. ''Now I want to talk to you, men. You are brave fellows, and patriotic ones too, but you are ignorant of this kind of work, and I am teaching you. I want you to observe that a good man on a good horse can never be caught. Another thing: cavalry can *trot* away from anything, and a gallop is a gait unbecoming a soldier, unless he is going toward the enemy. Remember that. We gallop toward the enemy, and trot away, always. Steady now! don't break ranks!''

And as the words left his lips a shell from a battery half a mile to the rear hissed over our heads.

''There,'' he resumed. ''I've been waiting for that, and watching those fellows. I knew they'd shoot too high, and I wanted you to learn how shells sound.''

We spent the next day or two literally within the Federal lines. We were shelled, skirmished with, charged, and surrounded scores of times, until we learned to hold in high regard our colonel's masterly skill in getting into and out of perilous positions. He seemed to blunder into them in sheer recklessness, but in getting out he showed us the quality of his genius; and before we reached Manassas, we had learned, among other things, to entertain a feeling closely akin to worship for our brilliant and daring leader. We had begun to understand, too, how much force he meant to give to his favorite dictum that the cavalry is the eye of the army.

His restless activity was one, at least, of the qualities which enabled him to win the reputation he achieved so rapidly. He could never be still. He was rarely ever in camp at all, and he never showed a sign of fatigue. He led almost everything. Even after he became a general officer, with well-nigh an army of horsemen under his command, I frequently followed him as my leader in a little party of half a dozen troopers, who might as well have gone with a sergeant on the duty assigned them; and once I was his only follower on a scouting expedition, of which he, a brigadier-general at the time, was the commander. I had been detailed to do some clerical work at his head-quarters, and, having finished the task assigned me, was waiting in the piazza of the house he occupied, for somebody to give me further orders, when Stuart came out.

"Is that your horse?" he asked, going up to the animal and examining him minutely.

I replied that he was, and upon being questioned further informed him that I did not wish to sell my steed. Turning to me suddenly, he said—

"Let's slip off on a scout, then; I'll ride your horse and you can ride mine. I want to try your beast's paces;" and mounting, we galloped away. Where or how far he intended to go I did not know. He was enamored of my horse, and rode, I suppose, for the pleasure of riding an animal which pleased him. We passed outside our picket line, and then, keeping in the woods, rode within that of the Union army. Wandering about in a purposeless way, we got a near view of some of the Federal camps, and finally finding ourselves objects of attention on the part of some well-mounted cavalry in blue uniforms, we rode rapidly down a road toward our own lines, our pursuers riding quite as rapidly immediately behind us.

"General," I cried presently, "there is a Federal picket post on the road just ahead of us. Had we not better oblique into the woods?"

"Oh no. They won't expect us from this direction, and we can ride over them before they make up their minds who we are."

Three minutes later we rode at full speed through the corporal's guard on picket, and were a hundred yards or more away before they could level a gun at us. Then half a dozen bullets whistled about our ears, but the cavalier paid no attention to them.

"Did you ever time this horse for a half-mile?" was all he had to say.

Expeditions of this singular sort were by no means uncommon occurrences with him. I am told by a friend who served on his staff, that he would frequently take one of his aids and ride away otherwise unattended into the enemy's lines; and oddly enough this was one of his ways of making friends with any officer to whom his rough, boyish ways had given offense. He would take the officer with him, and when they were alone would throw his arms around his companion, and say—

"My dear fellow, you mustn't be angry with me—you know I love you."

His boyishness was always apparent, and the affectionate nature of the man was hardly less so, even in public. He was especially fond of children, and I remember seeing him in the crowded waiting-room of the railroad station at Gordonsville with a babe on each arm; a great, bearded warrior, with his plumed hat, and with golden spurs clanking at his heels, engaged in a mad frolic with all the little people in the room, charging them right and left with the pair of babies which he had captured from their unknown mothers.

It was on the day of my ride with him that I heard him express his views of the war and his singular aspiration for himself. It was almost immediately after General McClellan assumed command of the army of the Potomac, and while we were rather eagerly expecting him to attack our strongly fortified position at Centreville. Stuart was talking with some members of his staff, with whom he had been wrestling a minute before. He said something about what they could do by way of amusement when they should go into winter-quarters.

"That is to say," he continued, "if George B. McClellan ever allows us to go into winter-quarters at all."

"Why, general? Do you think he will advance before spring?" asked one of the officers.

"Not against Centreville," replied the general. "He has too much sense for that, and I think he knows the shortest road to Richmond, too. If I am not greatly mistaken, we shall hear of him presently on his way up the James River."

In this prediction, as the reader knows, he was right. The conversation then passed to the question of results.

"I regard it as a foregone conclusion," said Stuart, "that we shall ultimately whip the Yankees. We are bound to believe that, anyhow; but the war is going to be a long and terrible one, first. We've only just begun it, and very few of us will see the end. *All I ask of fate is that I may be killed leading a cavalry charge.*"

The remark was not a boastful or seemingly insincere one. It was made quietly, cheerfully, almost eagerly, and it impressed me at the time with the feeling that the man's idea of happiness was what the French call glory, and that in his eyes there was no glory like that of dying in one of the tremendous onsets which he knew so well how to make. His wish was granted, as we know. He received his death-wound at the head of his troopers.

With those about him he was as affectionate as a woman, and his little boyish ways are remembered lovingly by those of his military household whom I have met since the war came to an end. On one occasion, just after a battle, he handed his coat to a member of his staff, saying—

"Try that on, captain, and see how it fits you."

The garment fitted reasonably well, and the general continued—

"Pull off two of the stars, and wear the coat to the war department, and tell the people there to make you a major."

The officer did as his chief bade him. Removing two of the three stars he made the coat a major's uniform, and the captain was promptly promoted in compliance with Stuart's request.

General Stuart was, without doubt, capable of handling an infantry command successfully, as he demonstrated at Chancellorsville, where he took Stonewall Jackson's place and led an army corps in a very severe engagement; but his special fitness was for cavalry service. His tastes were those of a horseman. Perpetual activity was a necessity of his existence, and he enjoyed nothing so much as danger. Audacity, his greatest virtue as a cavalry commander, would have been his besetting sin in any other position. Inasmuch as it is the business of the cavalry to live as constantly as possible within gunshot of the enemy, his recklessness stood him in excellent stead as a general of horse, but it is at least questionable whether his want of caution would not have led to disaster if his command had been of a less mobile sort. His critics say he was vain, and he was so, as a boy is. He liked to win the applause of his friends, and he liked still better to astonish the enemy, glorying in the thought that his foemen must admire his "impudence," as he called it, while they dreaded its manifestation. He was continually doing things of an extravagantly audacious sort, with no other purpose, seemingly, than that of making people stretch their eyes in wonder. He enjoyed the admiration of the enemy far more, I think, than he did that of his friends. This fact was evident in the care he took to make himself a conspicuous personage in every time of danger. He would ride at some distance from his men in a skirmish, and in every possible way attract a dangerous attention to himself. His slouch hat and long plume marked him in every battle, and made him a target for the riflemen to shoot at. In all this there was some vanity, if we choose to call it so, but it was an excellent sort of vanity for a cavalry chief to cultivate. I cannot learn that he ever boasted of any achievement, or that his vanity was ever satisfied with the things already done. His audacity was due, I think, to his sense of humor, not less than to his love of applause. He would laugh uproariously over the astonishment he imagined the Federal officers must feel after one of his peculiarly daring or sublimely impudent performances. When, after capturing a large number of horses and mules on one of his raids, he seized a telegraph station and sent a dispatch to General Meigs, then Quartermaster-General of the United States army, complaining that he could not afford to come after animals of so poor a quality, and urging that officer to provide better ones for capture in future, he enjoyed the joke quite as heartily as he did the success which made it possible.

The boyishness to which I have referred ran through every part of his character and every act of his life. His impetuosity in action, his love of military glory and of the military life, his occasional waywardness with his friends and his generous affection for them—all these were the traits of a great boy, full, to running over, of impulsive animal life. His audacity, too, which impressed strangers as the most marked feature of his character, was closely akin to that disposition which Dickens assures us is common to all boy-kind, to feel an insane delight in anything which specially imperils their necks. But the peculiarity showed itself most strongly in his love of uproarious fun. Almost at the beginning of the war he managed to surround himself with a number of persons whose principal qualification for membership of his military household was their ability to make fun. One of these was a noted banjo-player and ex-Negro minstrel. He played the banjo and sang comic songs to perfection, and *therefore* Stuart wanted him. I have known him to ride with his banjo, playing and singing, even on a march which might be changed at any moment into a battle; and Stuart's laughter on such occasions was sure to be heard as an accompaniment as far as the minstrel's voice could reach. He had another queer character about him, whose chief recommendation was his grotesque fierceness of appearance. This was Corporal Hagan, a very giant in frame, with an abnormal tendency to develop hair. His face was heavily bearded almost to his eyes, and his voice was as hoarse as distant thunder, which indeed it closely resembled. Stuart, seeing him in the ranks, fell in love with his peculiarities of person at once, and had him detailed for duty at head-quarters, where he made him a corporal, and gave him charge of the stables. Hagan, whose greatness was bodily only, was much elated by the attention shown him, and his person seemed to swell and his voice to grow deeper than ever under the influence of the newly acquired dignity of chevrons. All this was amusing, of course, and Stuart's delight was unbounded. The man remained with him till the time of his death, though not always as a corporal. In a mad freak of fun one day, the chief recommended his corporal for promotion, to see, he said, if the giant was capable of further swelling, and so the corporal became a lieutenant upon the staff.

With all his other boyish traits, Stuart had an almost child-like simplicity of character, and the combination of sturdy manhood with juvenile frankness and womanly tenderness of feeling made him a study to those who knew him best. His religious feeling was of that unquestioning, serene sort which rarely exists apart from the inexperience and the purity of women or children.

While I was serving in South Carolina, I met one evening the general commanding the military district, and he, upon learning that I had served with Stuart, spent the entire evening talking of his friend, for they two had been together in the old army before the war. He told me many anecdotes of the cavalier, nearly all of which turned in some way upon the generous boyishness of his character in some one or other of its phases. He said, among other things, that at one time, in winter-quarters on the plains of the West I think, he, Stuart, and another officer (one of those still living who commanded the army of the Potomac during the war) slept together in one bed, for several months. Stuart and his brother lieutenant, the general said, had a quarrel every night about some trifling thing or other, just as boys will, but when he had made all the petulant speeches he could, Stuart would lie still a while, and then, passing his arm around the neck of his comrade, would draw his head to his own breast and say some affectionate thing which healed all soreness of feeling and effectually restored the peace. During the evening's conversation this general formulated his opinion of Stuart's military character in very striking phrase.

"He is," he said, "the greatest cavalry officer that ever lived. He has all the dash, daring, and audacity of Murat, and a great deal more sense." It was his opinion, however, that there were men in both armies who would come to be known as greater cavalry men than Stuart, for the reason that Stuart used his men strictly as cavalry, while others would make dragoons of them. He believed that the nature of our country was much better adapted to dragoon than to cavalry service, and hence, while he thought Stuart the best of cavalry officers, he doubted his ability to stand against such men as General Sheridan, whose conception of the proper place of the horse in our war was a more correct one, he thought, than Stuart's. "To the popular mind," he went on to say, "every soldier who rides a horse is a cavalry man, and so Stuart will be measured by an incorrect standard. He will be classed with General Sheridan and measured by his success or the want of it. General Sheridan is without doubt the greatest of dragoon commanders, as Stuart is the greatest of cavalry men; but in this country dragoons are worth a good deal more than cavalry, and so General Sheridan will probably win the greater reputation. He will deserve it, too, because behind it is the sound judgment which tells him what use to make of his horsemen."

It is worthy of remark that all this was said before General Sheridan had made his reputation as an officer, and I remember that at the time his name was almost new to me.

From my personal experience and observation of General Stuart, as well as from the testimony of others, I am disposed to think that he attributed to every other man qualities and tastes like his own. Insensible to fatigue himself, he seemed never to understand how a well man could want rest; and as for hardship, there was nothing, in his view, which a man ought to enjoy quite so heartily, except danger. For a period of ten days, beginning before and ending after the first battle of Bull Run, we were not allowed once to take our saddles off. Night and day we were in the immediate presence of the enemy, catching naps when there happened for the moment to be nothing else to do, standing by our horses while they ate from our hands, so that we might slip their bridles on again in an instant in the event of a surprise, and eating such things as chance threw in our way, there being no rations anywhere within reach. After the battle, we were kept scouting almost continually for two days. We then marched to Fairfax Court House, and my company was again sent out in detachments on scouting expeditions in the neighborhood of Vienna and Falls Church. We returned to camp at sunset and were immediately ordered on picket. In the regular course of events we should have been relieved the next morning, but no relief came, and we were wholly without food. Another twenty-four hours passed, and still nobody came to take our place on the picket line. Stuart passed some of our men, however, and one of them asked him if he knew we had been on duty ten days, and on picket thirty-six hours without food.

"Oh nonsense!" he replied. "You don't look starved. There's a cornfield over there; jump the fence and get a good breakfast. You don't want to go back to camp, I know; it's stupid there, and all the fun is out here. I never go to camp if I can help it. Besides, I've kept your company on duty all this time as a compliment. You boys have acquitted yourselves too well to be neglected now, and I mean to give you a chance."

We thought this a jest at the time, but we learned afterwards that Stuart's idea of a supreme compliment to a company was its assignment to extra hazardous or extra fatiguing duty. If he observed specially good conduct on the part of a company, squad, or individual, he was sure to reward it by an immediate order to accompany him upon some unnecessarily perilous expedition.

His men believed in him heartily, and it was a common saying among them that "Jeb never says 'Go, boys,' but always 'Come, boys.' " We felt sure, too, that there was little prospect of excitement on any expedition of which he was not leader. If the scouting was to be merely a matter of form, promising nothing in the way of adventure, he would let us go by ourselves; but if there were prospect of "a fight or a race," as he expressed it, we were sure to see his long plume at the head of the column before we had passed outside our own line of pickets. While we lay in advance of Fairfax Court House, after Bull Run, Stuart spent more than a month around the extreme outposts on Mason's and Munson's hills without once coming to the camp of his command. When he wanted a greater force than he could safely detail from the companies on picket for the day, he would send after it, and with details of this kind he lived nearly all the time between the picket lines of the two armies. The outposts were very far in advance of the place at which we should have met and fought the enemy if an advance had been made, and so there was literally no use whatever in his perpetual scouting, which was kept up merely because the man could not rest. But aside from the fact that the cavalry was made up almost exclusively of the young men whose tastes and habits specially fitted them to enjoy this sort of service, Stuart's was one of those magnetic natures which always impress their own likeness upon others, and so it came to be thought a piece of good luck to be detailed for duty under his personal leadership. The men liked him and his ways, one of which was the pleasant habit he had of remembering our names and faces. I heard him say once that he knew by name not only every man in his old regiment, but every one also in the first brigade, and as I never knew him to hesitate for a name, I am disposed to believe that he did not exaggerate his ability to remember men. This and other like things served to make the men love him personally, and there can be no doubt that his skill in winning the affection of his troopers was one of the elements of his success. Certainly no other man could have got so much hard service out of men of their sort, without breeding discontent among them.

CHAPTER 7

LEE, JACKSON, AND SOME
LESSER WORTHIES

———————◆◆◆———————

THE story goes that when Napoleon thanked a private one day for some small service, giving him the complimentary title of "captain," the soldier replied with the question, "In what regiment, sire?" confident that this kind of recognition from the Little Corporal meant nothing less than a promotion, in any case; and while commanders are not ordinarily invested with Napoleon's plenary powers in such matters, military men are accustomed to value few things more than the favorable comments of their superiors upon their achievements or their capacity. And yet a compliment of the very highest sort, which General Scott paid Robert E. Lee, very nearly prevented the great Confederate from achieving a reputation at all. Up to the time of Virginia's secession, Lee was serving at Scott's headquarters, and when he resigned and accepted a commission from the governor of his native State, General Scott, who had already called him "the flower of the American army," pronounced him the best organizer in the country, and congratulated himself upon the fact that the Federal organization was already well under way before Lee began that of the Southern forces. This opinion, coming from the man who was recognized as best able to form a judgment on such a subject, greatly strengthened Lee's hand in the work he was then doing, and saved him the annoyance of dictation from people less skilled than he. But it nearly worked his ruin, for all that. The administration at Richmond was of too narrow a mold to understand that a man could be a master of more than one thing, and so, recognizing Lee's supreme ability as an organizer, the government seems to have assumed that he was good for very little else, and until the summer of 1862 he was carefully kept out of the way of all great military operations. When the two centres of strategic interest were at Winchester and Manassas, General Lee was kept in Western Virginia with a handful of raw troops, where he could not possibly accomplish anything for the cause, or even exercise the small share of fighting and strategic ability which the government was willing to believe he possessed. When there was no longer any excuse for keeping him there, he was disinterred, as it were, and reburied in the swamps of the South Carolina coast.

I saw him for the first time, in Richmond, at the very beginning of the war, dining with him at the house of a friend. He was then in the midst of his first popularity. He had begun the work of organization, and was everywhere recognized as the leader who was to create an army for us out of the volunteer material. I do not remember, with any degree of certainty, whether or not we expected him also to distinguish himself in the field, but as Mr. Davis and his personal followers were still in Montgomery, it is probable that the narrowness of their estimate of the chieftain was not yet shared by anybody in Richmond. Lee was at this time a young-looking, middle-aged man, with dark hair, dark moustache, and an otherwise smooth face, and a portrait taken then would hardly be recognized at all by those who knew him only after the cares and toils of war had furrowed his face and bleached his hair and beard. He was a model of manly beauty: large, well made, and graceful. His head was a noble one, and his countenance told, at a glance, of his high character and of that perfect balance of faculties, mental, moral, and physical, which constituted the chief element of his greatness. There was nothing about him which impressed one more than his eminent *robustness*, a quality no less marked in his intellect and his character than in his physical constitution. If his shapely person suggested a remarkable capacity for endurance, his manner, his countenance, and his voice quite as strongly hinted at the great soul which prompted him to take upon himself the responsibility for the Gettysburg campaign, when the people were loudest in their denunciations of the government as the author of that ill-timed undertaking.

I saw him next in South Carolina during the winter of 1861–62. He was living quietly at a little place called Coosawhatchie, on the Charleston and Savannah Railroad. He had hardly any staff with him, and was surrounded with none of the pomp and circumstance of war. His dress bore no marks of his rank, and hardly indicated even that he was a military man. He was much given to solitary afternoon rambles, and came almost every day to the camp of our battery, where he wandered alone and in total silence around the stables and through the gun park, much as a farmer curious as to cannon might have done. Hardly any of the men knew who he was, and one evening a sergeant, riding in company with a partially deaf teamster, met him in the road and saluted. The teamster called out to his companion, in a loud voice, after the manner of deaf people:

"I say, sergeant, who *is* that durned old fool? He's always a-pokin' round my hosses just as if he meant to steal one of 'em."

Certainly the honest fellow was not to blame for his failure to recognize, in the farmer-looking pedestrian, the chieftain who was shortly to win the greenest laurels the South had to give. During the following summer General Johnston's "bad habit of getting himself wounded" served to bring Lee to the front, and from that time till the end of the war he was the idol of army and people. The faith he inspired was simply marvelous. We knew very well that he was only a man, and very few of us would have disputed the abstract proposition that he was liable to err; but practically we believed nothing of the kind. Our confidence in his skill and his invincibility was absolutely unbounded. Our faith in his wisdom and his patriotism was equally perfect, and from the day on which he escorted McClellan to his gun-boats till the hour of his surrender at Appomattox, there was never a time when he might not have usurped all the powers of government without exciting a murmur. Whatever rank as a commander history may assign him, it is certain that no military chieftain was ever more perfect master than he of the hearts of his followers. When he appeared in the presence of troops he was sometimes cheered vociferously, but far more frequently his coming was greeted with a profound silence, which expressed much more truly than cheers could have done the well-nigh religious reverence with which the men regarded his person.

General Lee had a sententious way of saying things which made all his utterances peculiarly forceful. His language was always happily chosen, and a single sentence from his lips often left nothing more to be said. As good an example of this as any, perhaps, was his comment upon the military genius of General Meade. Not very long after that officer took command of the army of the Potomac, a skirmish occurred, and none of General Lee's staff officers being present, an acquaintance of mine was detailed as his personal aid for the day, and I am indebted to him for the anecdote. Some one asked our chief what he thought of the new leader on the other side, and in reply Lee said, "General Meade will commit no blunder in my front, and if I commit one he will make haste to take advantage of it." It is difficult to see what more he could have said on the subject.

I saw him for the last time during the war, at Amelia Court House, in the midst of the final retreat, and I shall never forget the heart-broken expression his face wore, or the still sadder tones of his voice as he gave me the instructions I had come to ask. The army was in utter confusion. It was already evident that we were being beaten back upon James River and could never hope to reach the Roanoke, on which stream alone there might be a possibility of making a stand. General Sheridan was harassing our broken columns at every step, and destroying us piecemeal. Worse than all, General Lee had been deserted by the terrified government in the very moment of his supreme need, and the food had been snatched from the mouths of the famished troops (as is more fully explained in another chapter) that the flight of the president and his followers might be hastened. The load put thus upon Lee's shoulders was a very heavy one for so conscientious a man as he to bear; and knowing, as every Southerner does, his habit of taking upon himself all blame for whatever went awry, we cannot wonder that he was sinking under the burden. His face was still calm, as it always was, but his carriage was no longer erect, as his soldiers had been used to see it. The troubles of those last days had already plowed great furrows in his forehead. His eyes were red as if with weeping; his cheeks sunken and haggard; his face colorless. No one who looked upon him then, as he stood there in full view of the disastrous end, can ever forget the intense agony written upon his features. And yet he was calm, self-possessed, and deliberate. Failure and the sufferings of his men grieved him sorely, but they could not daunt him, and his moral greatness was never more manifest than during those last terrible days. Even in the final correspondence with General Grant, Lee's manliness and courage and ability to endure lie on the surface, and it is not the least honorable thing in General Grant's history that he showed himself capable of appreciating the character of this manly foeman, as he did when he returned Lee's surrendered sword with the remark that he knew of no one so worthy as its owner to wear it.

After the war the man who had commanded the Southern armies remained master of all Southern hearts, and there can be no doubt that the wise advice he gave in reply to the hundreds of letters sent him prevented many mistakes and much suffering. The young men of the South were naturally disheartened, and a general exodus to Mexico, Brazil, and the Argentine Republic was seriously contemplated. General Lee's advice, "Stay at home, go to work, and hold your land," effectually prevented this saddest of all blunders; and his example was no less efficacious than his words, in recommending a diligent attention to business as the best possible cure for the evils wrought by the war.

From the chieftain who commanded our armies to his son and successor in the presidency of Washington-Lee University, the transition is a natural one; and, while it is my purpose, in these reminiscences, to say as little as possible of men still living, I may at least refer to General G. W. Custis Lee as the only man I ever heard of who tried to decline a promotion from brigadier to major general, for the reason that he thought there were others better entitled than he to the honor. I have it from good authority

that President Davis went in person to young Lee's head-
quarters to entreat a reconsideration of that officer's de-
termination to refuse the honor, and that he succeeded
with difficulty in pressing the promotion upon the singularly modest gentleman. Whether or not this younger Lee
has inherited his father's military genius we have no means
of knowing, but we are left in no uncertainty as to his
possession of his father's manliness and modesty, and personal worth.

Jackson was always a surprise. Nobody ever understood
him, and nobody has ever been quite able to account for
him. The members of his own staff, of whom I happen to
have known one or two intimately, seem to have failed,
quite as completely as the rest of the world, to penetrate
his singular and contradictory character. His biographer,
Mr. John Esten Cooke, read him more perfectly perhaps
than any one else, but even he, in writing of the hero, evi-
dently views him from the outside. Dr. Dabney, another
of Jackson's historians, gives us a glimpse of the man, in
one single aspect of his character, which may be a clew to
the whole. He says there are three kinds of courage, of
which two only are bravery. These three varieties of courage are, first, that of the man who is simply insensible of
danger; second, that of men who, understanding, appreciating, and fearing danger, meet it boldly nevertheless, from
motives of pride; and third, the courage of men keenly
alive to danger, who face it simply from a high sense of
duty.[1] Of this latter kind, the biographer tells us, was
Jackson's courage, and certainly there can be no better
clew to his character than this. Whatever other mysteries
there may have been about the man, it is clear that his

---

[1] As I have no copy of Dr. Dabney's work by me, and have seen none
for about ten years, I cannot pretend to quote the passage; but I
have given its substance in my own words.

well-nigh morbid devotion to duty was his ruling characteristic.

But nobody ever understood him fully, and he was a perpetual surprise to friend and foe alike. The cadets and the graduates of the Virginia Military Institute, who had known him as a professor there, held him in small esteem at the outset. I talked with many of them, and found no dissent whatever from the opinion that General Gilham and General Smith were the great men of the institute, and that Jackson, whom they irreverently nicknamed Tom Fool Jackson, could never be anything more than a martinet colonel, half soldier and half preacher. They were unanimous in prophesying his greatness after the fact, but of the two or three score with whom I talked on the subject at the beginning of the war, not one even suspected its possibility until after he had won his *sobriquet* "Stonewall" at Manassas.

It is natural enough that such a man should be credited in the end with qualities which he did not possess, and that much of the praise awarded him should be improperly placed; and in his case this seems to have been the fact. He is much more frequently spoken of as the great marcher than as the great fighter of the Confederate armies, and it is commonly said that he had an especial genius for being always on time. And yet General Lee himself said in the presence of a distinguished officer from whose lips I heard it, that Jackson was by no means so rapid a marcher as Longstreet, and that he had an unfortunate habit of *never being on time*. Without doubt he was, next to Lee, the greatest military genius we had, and his system of grand tactics was more Napoleonic than was that of any other officer on either side; but it would appear from this that while he has not been praised beyond his deserving, he has at least been commended mistakenly.

The affection his soldiers bore him has always been an enigma. He was stern and hard as a disciplinarian, cold in his manner, unprepossessing in appearance, and utterly lacking in the apparent enthusiasm which excites enthusiasm in others. He had never been able to win the affection of the cadets at Lexington, and had hardly won even their respect. And yet his soldiers almost worshiped him. Perhaps it was because he was so terribly in earnest, or it may have been because he was so generally successful—for there are few things men admire more than success—but whatever the cause was, no fact could be more evident than that Stonewall Jackson was the most enthusiastically loved man, except Lee, in the Confederate service, and that he shared with Lee the generous admiration even of his foes. His strong religious bent, his devotion to a form of religion the most gloomy—for his Calvinism amounted to very little less than fatalism, and his men called him "old blue-light" —his strictness of life, and his utter lack of vivacity and humor, would have been an impassable barrier between any other man and such troops as he commanded. He was Cromwell at the head of an army composed of men of the world, and there would seem to have been nothing in common between him and them; and yet Cromwell's psalm-singing followers never held their chief in higher regard or heartier affection than that with which these rollicking young planters cherished their sad-eyed and sober-faced leader. They even rejoiced in his extreme religiosity, and held it in some sort a work of supererogation, sufficient to atone for their own worldly-mindedness. They were never more devoted to him than when transgressing the very principles upon which his life was ordered; and when any of his men indulged in dram-drinking, a practice from which he always rigidly abstained, his health was sure to be the first toast given. On one occasion, a soldier who had imbibed enthusiasm with his whisky, feeling the inadequacy of the devotion shown by drinking to an absent chief, marched, canteen in hand, to Jackson's tent, and gaining admission proposed as a sentiment, "Here's to you, general! May I live to see you stand on the highest pinnacle of Mount Ararat, and hear you give the command, 'By the right of nations front into empires—worlds, right face!'"

I should not venture to relate this anecdote at all, did I not get it at first hand from an officer who was present at the time. It will serve, at least, to show the sentiments of extravagant admiration with which Jackson's men regarded him, whether it shall be sufficient to bring a smile to the reader's lips or not.

The first time I ever saw General Ewell, I narrowly missed making it impossible that there should ever be a *General* Ewell at all. He was a colonel then, and was in command of the camp of instruction at Ashland. I was posted as a sentinel, and my orders were peremptory to permit nobody to ride through the gate at which I was stationed. Colonel Ewell, dressed in a rough citizen's suit, without side-arms or other insignia of military rank, undertook to pass the forbidden portal. I commanded him to halt, but he cursed me instead, and attempted to ride over me. Drawing my pistol, cocking it, and placing its muzzle against his breast, I replied with more of vigor than courtesy in my speech, and forced him back, threatening and firmly intending to pull my trigger if he should resist in the least. He yielded himself to arrest, and I called the officer of the guard. Ewell was livid with rage, and ordered the officer to place me in irons at once, uttering maledictions upon me which it would not do to repeat here. The officer of the guard was a manly fellow, however, and refused even to remove me from the post.

"The sentinel has done only his duty," he replied, "and

if he had shot you, Colonel Ewell, you would have had only yourself to blame. I have here your written order that the sentinels at this gate shall allow nobody to pass through it on horseback, on any pretense whatever; and yet you come in citizen's clothes, a stranger to the guard, and try to ride him down when he insists upon obeying the orders you have given him.''

The sequel to the occurrence proved that, in spite of his infirm temper, Ewell was capable of being a just man, as he certainly was a brave one. He sent for me a little later, when he received his commission as a brigadier, and apologizing for the indignity with which he had treated me, offered me a desirable place upon his staff, which, with a still rankling sense of the injustice he had done me, I declined to accept.

General Ewell was at this time the most violently and elaborately profane man I ever knew. Elaborately, I say, because his profanity did not consist of single or even double oaths, but was ingeniously wrought into whole sentences. It was profanity which might be parsed, and seemed the result of careful study and long practice. Later in the war he became a religious man, but before that time his genius for swearing was phenomenal. An anecdote is told of him, for the truth of which I cannot vouch, but which certainly is sufficiently characteristic to be true. It is said that on one occasion, the firing having become unusually heavy, a chaplain who had labored to convert the general, or at least to correct the aggressive character of his wickedness, remarked that as he could be of no service where he was, he would seek a less exposed place, whereupon Ewell remarked:

''Why, chaplain, you're the most inconsistent man I ever saw. You say you're anxious to get to heaven above all things, and now that you've got the best chance you

ever had to go, you run away from it just as if you'd
rather not make the trip, after all.''

I saw nothing of General Ewell after he left Ashland,
early in the summer of 1861, until I met him in the winter
of 1864-65. Some enormous rifled guns had been mounted
at Chaffin's Bluff, below Richmond, and I went from my
camp near by to see them tested. General Ewell was present,
and while the firing was in progress he received a dispatch
saying that the Confederates had been victorious in an
engagement between Mackey's Point and Pocotaligo. As no
State was mentioned in the dispatch, and the places named
were obscure ones, General Ewell was unable to guess in
what part of the country the action had been fought. He
read the dispatch aloud, and asked if any one present could
tell him where Mackey's Point and Pocotaligo were. Having served for a considerable time on the coast of South
Carolina, I was able to give him the information he sought.
When I had finished he looked at me intently for a moment,
and then asked, ''Aren't you the man who came so near
shooting me at Ashland?''

I replied that I was.

''I'm very glad you didn't do it,'' he said.

''So am I,'' I replied; and that was all that was said
on either side.

The queerest of all the military men I met or saw during
the war was General W. H. H. Walker, of Georgia. I saw
very little of him, but that little impressed me strongly.
He was a peculiarly belligerent man, and if he could have
been kept always in battle he would have been able doubtless to keep the peace as regarded his fellows and his superiors. As certain periods of inaction are necessary in all
wars, however, General Walker was forced to maintain a
state of hostility toward those around and above him. During the first campaign he got into a newspaper war with

the president and Mr. Benjamin, in which he handled both of those gentlemen rather roughly, but failing to move them from the position they had taken with regard to his promotion—that being the matter in dispute,—he resigned his commission, and took service as a brigadier-general under authority of the governor of Georgia. In this capacity he was at one time in command of the city of Savannah, and it was there that I saw him for the first and only time, just before the reduction of Fort Pulaski by General Gilmore. The reading-room of the Pulaski House was crowded with guests of the hotel and evening loungers from the city, when General Walker came in. He at once began to talk, not so much to the one or two gentlemen with whom he had just shaken hands, as to the room full of strangers and the public generally. He spoke in a loud voice and with the tone and manner of a bully and a braggart, which I am told he was not at all.

"You people are very brave at arms-length," he said, "provided it is a good long arms-length. You aren't a bit afraid of the shells fired at Fort Pulaski, and you talk as boldly as Falstaff over his sack, now. But what will you do when the Yankee gun-boats come up the river and begin to throw hot shot into Savannah? I know what you'll do. You'll get dreadfully uneasy about your plate-glass mirrors and your fine furniture; and I give you fair warning now that if you want to save your mahogany you'd better be carting it off up country at once, for I'll never surrender anything more than the ashes of Savannah. I'll stay here, and I'll keep you here, till every shingle burns and every brick gets knocked into bits the size of my thumbnail, and then I'll send the Yankees word that there isn't any Savannah to surrender. Now I mean this, every word of it. But you don't believe it, and the first time a gun-boat comes in sight you'll all come to me and say, 'General, we can't fight gun-boats with any hope of success,—don't you think we'd better surrender?' Do you know what I'll do then? I've had a convenient limb trimmed up, on the tree in front of my head-quarters, and I'll string up every man that dares say surrender, or anything else beginning with an *s*.''

And so he went on for an hour or more, greatly to the amusement of the crowd. I am told by those who knew him best that his statement of his purposes was probably not an exaggerated one, and that if he had been charged with the defense of the city against a hostile fleet, he would have made just such a resolute resistance as that which he promised. His courage and endurance had been abundantly proved in Mexico, at any rate, and nobody who knew him ever doubted either.

Another queer character, though in a very different way, was General Ripley, who for a long time commanded the city of Charleston. He was portly in person, of commanding and almost pompous presence, and yet, when one came to know him, was as easy and unassuming in manner as if he had not been a brigadier-general at all. I had occasion to call upon him officially, a number of times, and this afforded me an excellent opportunity to study his character and manners. On the morning after the armament of Fort Ripley was carried out to the Federal fleet by the crew of the vessel on which it had been placed, I spent an hour or two in General Ripley's head-quarters, waiting for something or other, though I have quite forgotten what. I amused myself looking through his telescope at objects in the harbor. Presently I saw a ship's launch, bearing a white flag, approach Fort Sumter. I mentioned the matter to my companion, and General Ripley, overhearing the remark, came quickly to the glass. A moment later he said to his signal operator—

''Tell Fort Sumter if that's a Yankee boat to burst her

wide open, flag or no flag.'' The message had no sooner gone, however, than it was recalled, and instructions more in accordance with the rules of civilized warfare substituted.

General Ripley stood less upon rule and held red tape in smaller regard than any other brigadier I ever met. My company was at that time an independent battery, belonging to no battalion and subject to no intermediate authority between that of its captain and that of the commanding general. It had but two commissioned officers on duty, and I, as its sergeant-major, acted as a sort of adjutant, making my reports directly to General Ripley's headquarters. One day I reported the fact that a large part of our harness was unfit for further use.

''Well, why don't you call a board of survey and have it condemned?'' he asked.

''How can we, general? We do not belong to any battalion, and so have nobody to call the board or to compose it, either.''

''Let your captain call it then, and put your own officers on it.''

''But we have only one officer, general, besides the captain, and there must be three on the board, while the officer calling it cannot be one of them.''

''Oh, the deuce!'' he replied. ''What's the difference? The harness ain't fit for use and there's plenty of new in the arsenal. Let your captain call a board consisting of the lieutenant and you and a sergeant. It ain't legal, of course, to put any but commissioned officers on, but I tell you to do it, and one pair of shoulder-straps is worth more now than a court-house full of habeas corpuses. Write 'sergeant' so that nobody can read it, and I'll make my clerks mistake it for 'lieutenant' in copying. Get your board together, go on to say that after a due examination, and all that, the board respectfully reports that it finds the said harness not worth a damn, or words to that effect; send in your report and I'll approve it, and you'll have a new set of harness in three days. What's the use of pottering around with technicalities when the efficiency of a battery is at stake? We're not lawyers, but soldiers.''

The speech was a peculiarly characteristic one, and throughout his administration of affairs in Charleston, General Ripley showed this disposition to promote the good of the service at the expense of routine. He was not a good martinet, but he was a brave, earnest man and a fine officer, of a sort of which no army can have too many.

CHAPTER 8

SOME QUEER PEOPLE

———— ◄•► ————

GENERALS would be of small worth, indeed, if there were no lesser folk than they in service, and the interesting people one meets in an army do not all wear sashes, by any means. The composition of the battery in which I served for a considerable time afforded me an opportunity to study some rare characters, of a sort not often met with in ordinary life, and as these men interested me beyond measure, I have a mind to sketch a few of them here in the hope that their oddities may prove equally entertaining to my readers.

In the late autumn of 1861, after a summer with Stuart, circumstances, with an explanation of which it is not necessary now to detain the reader, led me to seek a transfer to a light battery, in which I was almost an entire stranger. When I joined this new command, the men were in a state of partial mutiny, the result of a failure to receive their pay and clothing allowance. The trouble was that there was no one in the battery possessed of sufficient clerical skill to make out a proper muster and pay roll. Several efforts had been made, but to no purpose, and when I arrived the camp was in a state of turmoil. The men were for the most part illiterate mountaineers, and no explanations which the officers were able to give served to disabuse their minds of the thought that they were being swindled in some way. Learning what the difficulty was, I volunteered my services for the clerical work required, and two hours after my arrival I had the pleasure of paying off the men and restoring peace to the camp. Straightway the captain made me sergeant-major, and the men wanted to make me captain. The popularity won thus in the outset served me many a good turn, not the least of which I count the opportunity it gave me to study the characters of the men, whose confidant and adviser I became in all matters of difficulty. I deciphered the letters they received from home and wrote replies from their dictation, and there were parts of this correspondence which would make my fortune as a humorous writer, if I could reproduce here the letters received now and then.

The men, as I have said, were for the most part illiterate mountaineers, with just a sufficient number of educated gentlemen among them (mostly officers and non-commissioned officers) to join each other in a laugh at the oddity of the daily life in the camp. The captain had been ambitious at one time of so increasing the company as to make a battalion of it, and to that end had sought recruits in all quarters. Among others he had enlisted seven genuine ruffians whom he had found in a Richmond jail, and who enlisted for the sake of a release from durance. These men formed a little clique by themselves, a sort of miniature New York sixth ward society, which afforded me a singularly interesting social study, of a kind rarely met with by any but home missionaries and police authorities. There were enough of them to form a distinct criminal class, so that I had opportunity to study their life as a whole, and not merely the phenomena presented by isolated specimens.

All of these seven men had seen service somewhere, and except as regarded turbulence and utter unmanageability they were excellent soldiers. Jack Delaney, or "one-eyed Jack Delaney," as he was commonly called, was a tall, muscular, powerful fellow, who had lost an eye in a street fight, and was quite prepared to sacrifice the other in the same way at any moment. Tommy Martin was smaller and plumper than Jack, but not one whit less muscular or less desperately belligerent. Tim Considine was simply a beauty. He was not more than twenty-one years of age, well-built, with a fair, pearly, pink and white complexion, regular features, exquisite eyes, and a singularly shapely and well-poised head. His face on any woman's shoulders would have made her a beauty and a belle in a Brooklyn drawing-room. I group these three together because they are associated with each other in my mind. They messed together and occupied one tent. Never a day passed which brought with it no battle royal between two or all three of them. These gentlemen—for that is what they uniformly called themselves, though they pronounced the word "gints"—were born in Baltimore. I have their word for this, else I should never have suspected the fact. Their names were of Hibernian mold. They spoke the English language with as pretty a brogue as ever echoed among the hills of Galway. They were much given to such expletives as "faith" and "be me sowl," and "be jabers," and moreover they were always "afther" doing something; but they were born in Baltimore, nevertheless, for they solemnly told me so.

I am wholly unable to give the reader any connected account of the adventures and life struggles through which these men had passed, for the reason that I was never able to win their full and unreserved confidence; but I caught glimpses of their past, here and there, from which I think it safe to assume that their personal histories had been of a dramatic, not to say of a sensational sort. My battery was sent one day to Bee's Creek, on the South Carolina coast, to meet an anticipated advance of the enemy. No enemy came, however, and we lay there on the sand, under a scorching sub-tropical sun, in a swarm of sand-flies so dense that many of our horses died of their stings, while neither sleep nor rest was possible to the men. A gun-boat lay just out of reach beyond a point in the inlet, annoying us by throwing at us an occasional shell of about the size and shape of a street lamp. Having a book with me I sought a place under a caisson for the sake of the shade, and spent an hour or two in reading. While I was there, Jack Delaney and Tommy Martin, knowing nothing of my presence, took seats on the ammunition chests, and fell to talking.

"An' faith, Tommy," said Jack, "an' it isn't this sort of foightin' I'm afther loikin' at all, bad luck to it."

"An' will ye tell me, Jack," said his companion, "what sort of foightin' it is, ye loikes?"

"Ah, Tommy, it's mesilf that loikes the raal foightin'. Give me an open sea, an' *close quarthers,* an' a *black flag,* Tommy, an' that's the sort of foightin' I'm afther loikin', sure."

"A - an' I believe it's a poirate ye are, Jack."

"You're roight, Tommy; it's a poirate I am, ivery inch o' me!"

Here was a glimpse of the man's character which proved also a hint of his life story, as I afterwards learned. He had been a pirate, and an English court, discovering the fact, had "ordered his funeral," as he phrased it, but by some means or other he had secured a pardon on condition of his enlistment in the British navy, from which he had deserted at the first opportunity. Jack was very much devoted to his friends, and especially to those above him in

social or military rank; and a more loyal fellow I never
knew. The captain of the battery and I were tent mates
and mess mates, and although we kept a competent Negro
servant, Jack insisted upon blacking our boots, stretching
our tent, brushing our clothes, looking after our fire, and
doing a hundred other services of the sort, for which he
could never be persuaded to accept compensation of any
kind.

When we arrived in Charleston for the first time, on
our way to the post assigned us at Coosawhatchie, we were
obliged to remain a whole day in the city, awaiting transportation. Knowing the temper of our "criminal class,"
we were obliged to confine all the men strictly within camp
boundaries, lest our Baltimore Irishmen and their fellows
should get drunk and give us trouble. We peremptorily refused to let any of the men pass the line of sentinels, but
Jack Delaney, being in sad need of a pair of boots, was
permitted to go into the city in company with the captain. That officer guarded him carefully, and as they were
returning to camp the captain, thinking that there could
be no danger in allowing the man one dram, invited him
to drink at a hotel counter.

"Give us your very best whisky," he said to the man
behind the bar; whereupon that functionary placed a decanter and two glasses before them.

Jack's one eye flashed fire instantly, and jumping upon
the counter he screamed, "What d' ye mean, ye bloody spal-
peen, by insultin' me captain in that way? I'll teach ye
your manners, ye haythen." The captain could not guess
the meaning of the Irishman's wrath, but he interfered for
the protection of the frightened servitor, and asked Jack
what he meant.

"What do I mean? An' sure an' I mean to break his
bit of a head, savin' your presence, captain. I'll teach him

not to insult me captain before me very eyes, by givin'
him the same bottle he gives Jack Delaney to drink out of.
An' sure an' me moother learnt me betther manners nor to
presume to drink from the same bottle with me betthers.''

The captain saved the bar-tender from the effects of
Jack's wrath, but failed utterly to convince that well-bred
Irish gentleman that no offense against good manners had
been committed. He refused to drink from the ''captain's
bottle,'' and a separate decanter was provided for him.

On another occasion Jack went with one of the officers
to a tailor's shop, and, without apparent cause, knocked
the knight of the shears down and was proceeding to beat
him, when the officer commanded him to desist.

''An' sure if your honor says he's had enough, I'll quit,
but I'd loike to murdher him.''

Upon being questioned as to the cause of his singular behavior, he explained that the tailor had shown unpardon-
ably bad manners by keeping his hat on his head while
taking the lieutenant's measure.

These men were afraid of nothing and respected nothing
but rank; but their regard for that was sufficiently exaggerated perhaps to atone for their short-comings in other respects. A single chevron on a man's sleeve made them at
once his obedient servants, and never once, even in their
cups, did they resist constituted authority, directly asserted.
For general rules they had no respect whatever. Anything
which assumed the form of law they violated as a matter of
course, if not, as I suspect, as a matter of conscience; but
the direct command of even a corporal was held binding
always. Jack Delaney, who never disobeyed any order de
livered to him in person, used to swim the Ashley River
every night, at imminent risk of being eaten by sharks,
chiefly because it was a positive violation of orders to cross
at all from our camp on Wappoo Creek to Charleston.

Tommy Martin and Tim Considine were bosom friends, and inseparable companions. They fought each other frequently, but these little episodes worked no ill to their friendship. One day they quarreled about something, and Considine, drawing a huge knife from his belt, rushed upon Martin with evident murderous intent. Martin, planting himself firmly, dealt his antagonist a blow exactly between the eyes, which laid him at full length on the ground. I ran at once to command the peace, but before I got to the scene of action I heard Considine call out, from his supine position—

"Bully for you, Tommy! I niver knew a blow better delivered in me loife!" And that ended the dispute.

One night, after taps, a fearful hubbub arose in the Irish quarter of the camp, and running to the place, the captain, a corporal, and I managed to separate the combatants; but as Jack Delaney had a great butcher knife in his hands with which it appeared he had already severely cut another Irishman, Dan Gorman by name, we thought it best to bind him with a prolonge. He submitted readily, lying down on the ground to be tied. While we were drawing the rope around him, Gorman, a giant in size and strength, leaned over us and dashed a brick with all his force into the prostrate man's face. Had it struck his skull it must have killed him instantly, as indeed we supposed for a time that it had.

"What do you mean by that, sir?" asked the captain, seizing Gorman by the collar.

Pointing to a fearful gash in his own neck, the man replied—

"Don't ye see I'm a dead man, captain? An' sure an' *do ye think I'm goin' to hell widout me pardner?*"

The tone of voice in which the question was asked clearly indicated that in his view nothing could possibly be more utterly preposterous than such a supposition.

Charley Lear belonged to this party, though he was not a Celt, but an Englishman. Charley was a tailor by trade and a desperado in practice. He had kept a bar in Vicksburg, had dug gold in California, and had "roughed it" in various other parts of the world. His was a scarred breast, showing seven knife thrusts and the marks of two bullets, one of which had passed entirely through him. And yet he was in perfect health and strength. He was a man of considerable intelligence and fair education, whose association with ruffians was altogether a matter of choice. He was in no sense a criminal, I think, and while I knew him, at least, was perfectly peaceful. But he liked rough company and sought it diligently, taking the consequences when they came. He professed great regard and even affection for me, because I had done him a rather important service once.

Finding it impossible to govern these men without subjecting the rest of the company to a much severer discipline than was otherwise necessary or desirable, we secured the transfer of our ruffians to another command in the fall of 1862, and I saw no more of any of them until after the close of the war. I went into a tailor's shop in Memphis one day, during the winter of 1865–66, to order a suit of clothing. After selecting the goods I was asked to step up-stairs to be measured. While the cutter was using his tape upon me, one of the journeymen on the great bench at the end of the room suddenly dropped his work, and, bounding forward, literally clasped me in his arms, giving me a hug which a grizzly bear might be proud of. It was Charley Lear, of course, and I had the utmost difficulty in refusing his offer to pay for the goods and make my clothes himself without charge.

Our assortment of queer people was a varied one, and among the rest there were two ex-circus actors, Jack Hawkins and Colonel Denton, to wit. Hawkins was an inoffensive and even a timid fellow, whose delight it was to sing bold robber songs in the metallic voice peculiar to vocalists of the circus. There was something inexpressibly ludicrous in the constrast between the bloody-mindedness of his songs and the gentle shyness and timidity of the man who sang them. Everybody domineered over him, and he was especially oppressed in the presence of our other ex-clown, whose assumption of superior wisdom and experience often overpowered stronger men than poor John Hawkins ever was. Denton was one of those men who are sure, in one way or another, to become either "colonel" or "judge." He was sixty-five years old when I first knew him, and had been "the colonel" longer than anybody could remember. He was of good parentage, and until he ran away with a circus at the age of eleven had lived among genteel people. His appearance and manner were imposing always, and never more so than when he was drunk. He buttoned his coat with the air of a man who is about to ride over broad ancestral acres, and ate his dinner, whatever it might consist of, with all the dignity of a host who does his guests great honor in entertaining them. He was an epicure in his tastes, of course, and delighted to describe peculiarly well-prepared dinners which he said he had eaten in company with especially distinguished gentlemen. He was an expert, too, he claimed, in the preparation of salads and the other arts of a like nature in which fine gentlemen like to excel even professional cooks. When rations happened to be more than ordinarily limited in quantity or worse than usual in quality, Denton was sure to visit various messes while they were at dinner, and regale them with a highly wrought description of an imaginary feast from which he would profess to have risen ten minutes before.

"You ought to have dined with me to-day," he would say. "I had a deviled leg of turkey, and some beautiful broiled oysters with Spanish olives. I never eat broiled oysters without olives. You try it sometime, and you'll never regret it. Then I had a stuffed wild goose's liver. Did you ever eat one? Well, you don't know what a real titbit is, then. Not stuffed in the ordinary way, but stuffed scientifically and cooked in a way you never saw it done before.'' And thus he would go on, naming impossible viands and describing preposterous processes of cookery, until ''cooked in a way you never saw it done before'' became a proverb in the camp. The old sinner would do all this on an empty stomach too, and I sometimes fancied he found in the delights of his imaginary banquets some compensation for the short rations and hard fare of his actual experience.

He was in his glory, however, only when he was away from camp and among strangers. He always managed to impress people who didn't know him with his great wealth and prominence. I overheard him once, in the office of the Charleston Hotel, inviting some gentlemen to visit and dine with him.

''Come out this evening,'' he said, ''to my place in Charleston Neck, and take a bachelor dinner with me. I've just got some duck from Virginia—canvas-back, you know—and my steward will be sure to have something else good on hand. I've got some good madeira too, that I imported myself. Now you'll not disappoint me, will you? And after dinner we'll have a turn at billiards: I've just had my tables overhauled. But you'll have to excuse me long enough now for me to ride down and tell the major to take care of things in camp till morning.''

And with that he gave them an address in the aristocratic quarter of Charleston, leaving them to meditate upon the good luck they had fallen upon in meeting this wealthy and hospitable ''colonel.''

Denton was an inveterate gambler, and was in the habit

of winning a good deal of money from the men after pay-
day. One day he gave some sound advice to a young man
from whom he had just taken a watch in settlement of a
score.

"Now let me give you some advice, Bill," he said. "I've
seen a good deal of this kind of thing, and I know what I'm
talking about. You play fair now, and you always lose.
You'll win after a while if you keep on, but I tell you, Bill,
nobody ever can win at cards without cheating. You'll cheat
a little after a while, and you'll cheat a good deal before
you've done with it. You'd better quit now, while you're
honest, because you'll cheat if you keep on, and when a man
cheats at cards he'll steal, Bill. *I speak from experience.*"
All of which impressed me as a singularly frank confession
under the circumstances.

Among other odd specimens we had in our battery the
most ingenious malingerer I ever heard of. He was in service
four years, drew his pay regularly, was of robust frame
and in perfect health always, and yet during the whole time
he was never off the sick-list for a single day. His capacity
to endure contempt was wholly unlimited, else he would
have been shamed by the gibes of the men, the sneers of the
surgeons, and the denunciations of the officers, into some
show, at least, of a disposition to do duty. He spent the
greater part of his time in hospital, never staying in camp
a moment longer than he was obliged to do. When discharged, as a well man, from one hospital, he would start
toward his command, and continue in that direction till he
came to another infirmary, when he would have a relapse at
once, and gain admission there. Discharged again he would
repeat the process at the next hospital, and one day near the
end of the war he counted up something like a hundred
different post and general hospitals of which he had been
an inmate, while he had been admitted to some of them more

than half a dozen times each. The surgeons resorted to a variety of expedients by which to get rid of him. They burned his back with hot coppers; gave him the most nauseous mixtures; put him on the lowest possible diet; treated him to cold shower-baths four or five times daily; and did everything else they could think of to drive him from the hospitals, but all to no purpose. In camp it was much the same. On the morning after his arrival from hospital he would wake up with some totally new ache, and report himself upon the sick-list. There was no way by which to conquer his obstinacy, and, as I have said, he escaped duty to the last.

Another curious case, and one which is less easily explained, was that of a much more intelligent man, who for more than a year feigned every conceivable disease, in the hope that he might be discharged the service. One or two of us amused ourselves with his case, by mentioning in his presence the symptoms of some disease of which he had never heard, the surgeon furnishing us the necessary information, and in every case he had the disease within less than twenty-four hours. Finally, and this was the oddest part of the matter, he gave up the attempt, recovered his health suddenly, and became one of the very best soldiers in the battery, a man always ready for duty, and always faithful in its discharge. He was made a corporal and afterwards a sergeant, and there was no better in the battery.

CHAPTER 9

RED TAPE

————◂•▸————

T HE history of the Confederacy, when it shall be fully and fairly written, will appear the story of a dream to those who shall read it, and there are parts of it at least which already seem a nightmare to those of us who helped make it. Founded upon a constitution which jealously withheld from it nearly all the powers of government, without even the poor privilege of existing beyond the moment when some one of the States composing it should see fit to put it to death, the Richmond government nevertheless grew speedily into a despotism, and for four years wielded absolute power over an obedient and uncomplaining people. It tolerated no questioning, brooked no resistance, listened to no remonstrance. It levied taxes of an extraordinary kind upon a people already impoverished almost to the point of starvation. It made of every man a soldier, and extended indefinitely every man's term of enlistment. Under pretense of enforcing the conscription law it established an oppressive system of domiciliary visits. To preserve order and prevent desertion it instituted and maintained a system of guards and passports, not less obnoxious, certainly, than the worst thing of the sort ever devised by the most paternal of despotisms. In short, a government constitutionally weak beyond all precedent was able for four years to exercise in a particularly offensive way all the powers of absolutism, and that, too, over a people who had been living under republican rule for generations. That such a thing was possible seems at the first glance a marvel, but the reasons for it are not far to seek. Despotisms usually ground themselves upon the theories of extreme democracy, for one thing, and in this case the consciousness of the power to dissolve and destroy the government at will made the people tolerant of its encroachments upon personal and State rights; the more especially, as the presiding genius of the despotism was the man who had refused a promotion to the rank of brigadier-general of volunteers during the Mexican war, on the ground that the general government could not grant such a commission without violating the rights of a State. The despotism of a government presided over by a man so devoted as he to State rights seemed less dangerous than it might otherwise have appeared. His theory was so excellent that people pardoned his practice. It is of some parts of that practice that we shall speak in the present chapter.

Nothing could possibly be idler than speculation upon what might have been accomplished with the resources of the South if they had been properly economized and wisely used. And yet every Southern man must feel tempted to indulge in some such speculation whenever he thinks of the subject at all, and remembers, as he must, how shamefully those resources were wasted and how clumsily they were handled in every attempt to use them in the prosecution of the war. The army was composed, as we have seen in a previous chapter, of excellent material; and under the influence of field service it soon became a very efficient body of well-drilled and well-disciplined men. The skill of its leaders is a matter of history, too well known to need comment here.

But the government controlling army and leaders was both passively and actively incompetent in a surprising degree. It did, as nearly as possible, *all* those things which it ought not to have done, at the same time developing a really marvelous genius for leaving undone those things which it ought to have done. The story of its incompetence and its presumption, if it could be adequately told, would read like a romance. Its weakness paralyzed the army and people, and its weakness was the less hurtful side of its character. Its full capacity for ill was best seen in the extraordinary strength it developed whenever action of a wrong-headed sort could work disaster, and the only wonder is that with such an administration at its back the Confederate army was able to keep the field at all. I have already had occasion to explain that the sentiment of the South made it the duty of every man who could bear arms to go straight to the front and to stay there. The acceptance of any less actively military position than that of a soldier in the field was held to be little less than a confession of cowardice; and cowardice, in the eyes of the Southerners, is the one sin which may not be pardoned either in this world or the next. The strength of this sentiment it is difficult for anybody who did not live in its midst to conceive, and its effect was to make worthy men spurn everything like civic position. To go where the bullets were whistling was the one course open to gentlemen who held their honor sacred and their reputation dear. And so the offices in Richmond and elsewhere, the bureaus of every sort, on the proper conduct of which so much depended, were filled with men willing to be sneered at as dwellers in "bomb-proofs" and holders of "life insurance policies."

Nor were the petty clerkships the only positions which brought odium upon their incumbents. If an able-bodied man accepted even a seat in Congress, he did so at peril of his reputation for patriotism and courage, and very many of the men whose wisdom was most needed in that body positively refused to go there at the risk of losing a chance to be present with their regiments in battle. Under the circumstances, no great degree of strength or wisdom was to be looked for at the hands of Congress, and certainly that assemblage of gentlemen has never been suspected of showing much of either; while the administrative machinery presided over by the small officials and clerks who crowded Richmond was at once a wonder of complication and a marvel of inefficiency.

But, if we may believe the testimony of those who were in position to know the facts, the grand master of incapacity, whose hand was felt everywhere, was President Davis himself. Not content with perpetually meddling in the smallest matters of detail, and prescribing the petty routine of office work in the bureau, he interfered, either directly or through his personal subordinates, with military operations which no man, not present with the army, could be competent to control, and which he, probably, was incapable of justly comprehending in any case. With the history of his quarrels with the generals in the field, and the paralyzing effect they had upon military operations, the public is already familiar. Leaving things of that nature to the historian, I confine myself to smaller matters, my purpose being merely to give the reader an idea of the experiences of a Confederate soldier, and to show him Confederate affairs as they looked when seen from the inside.

I can hardly hope to make the ex-soldier of the Union understand fully how we on the other side were fed in the field. He fought and marched with a skilled commissariat at his back, and, for his further staff of comfort, had the Christian and Sanitary commissions, whose handy tin cups and other camp conveniences came to us only through the

uncertain and irregular channel of abandonment and capture; and unless his imagination be a vivid one, he will not
easily conceive the state of our commissariat or the privations we suffered as a consequence of its singularly bad
management. The first trouble was, that we had for a
commissary-general a crotchety doctor, some of whose acquaintances had for years believed him insane. Aside from
his suspected mental aberration, and the crotchets which
had made his life already a failure, he knew nothing whatever of the business belonging to the department under his
control, his whole military experience having consisted of
a few years' service as a lieutenant of cavalry in one of the
Territories, many years before the date of his appointment
as chief of subsistence in the Confederacy. Wholly without
experience to guide him, he was forced to evolve from his
own badly balanced intellect whatever system he should
adopt, and from the beginning of the war until the early
part of the year 1865, the Confederate armies were forced
to lean upon this broken reed in the all-important matter
of a food supply. The generals commanding in the field, we
are told on the very highest authority, protested, suggested,
remonstrated almost daily, but their remonstrances were
unheeded and their suggestions set at naught. At Manassas,
where the army was well-nigh starved out in the very beginning of the war, food might have been abundant but for
the obstinacy of this one man. On our left lay a country un-
surpassed, and almost unequaled, in productiveness. It was
rich in grain and meat, these being its special products. A
railroad, with next to nothing to do, penetrated it, and its
stores of food were nearly certain to be exposed to the
enemy before any other part of the country should be con-
quered. The obvious duty of the commissary-general, therefore, was to draw upon that section for the supplies which
were both convenient and abundant. The chief of sub-

sistence ruled otherwise, however, thinking it better to let that source of supply lie exposed to the first advance of the enemy, while he drew upon the Richmond *dépôts* for a daily ration, and shipped it by the overtasked line of railway leading from the capital to Manassas. It was nothing to him that he was thus exhausting the rear and crippling the resources of the country for the future. It was nothing to him that in the midst of plenty the army was upon a short allowance of food. It was nothing that the shipments of provisions from Richmond by this railroad seriously interfered with other important interests. System was everything, and this was a part of his system. The worst of it was, that in this all-important branch of the service experience and organization wrought little if any improvement as the war went on, so that as the supplies and the means of transportation grew smaller, the undiminished inefficiency of the department produced disastrous results. The army, suffering for food, was disheartened by the thought that the scarcity was due to the exhaustion of the country's resources. Red tape was supreme, and no sword was permitted to cut it. I remember one little circumstance, which will serve to illustrate the absoluteness with which system was suffered to override sense in the administration of the affairs of the subsistence department. I served for a time on the coast of South Carolina, a country which produces rice in great abundance, and in which fresh pork and mutton might then be had almost for the asking, while the climate is wholly unsuited to the making of flour or bacon. Just at that time, however, the officials of the commissary department saw fit to feed the whole army on bacon and flour, articles which, if given to troops in that quarter of the country at all, must be brought several hundred miles by rail. The local commissary officers made various suggestions looking to the use of the provisions of which the country round about was full, but, so

far as I could learn, no attention whatever was paid to
them. At the request of one of these post commissaries, I
wrote an elaborate and respectful letter on the subject,
setting forth the fact that rice, sweet potatoes, corn meal,
hominy, grits, mutton, and pork existed in great abundance
in the immediate neighborhood of the troops, and could be
bought for less than one third the cost of the flour and
bacon we were eating. The letter was signed by the post
commissary, and forwarded through the regular channels,
with the most favorable indorsements possible, but it resulted in nothing. The department presently found it impossible to give us full rations of bacon and flour, but it
still refused to think of the remedy suggested. It cut down
the ration instead, thus reducing the men to a state of semi-
starvation in a country full of food. Relief came at last in
the shape of a technicality, else it would not have been
allowed to come at all. A vigilant captain discovered that
the men were entitled by law to commutation in money for
their rations, at fixed rates, and acting upon this the men
were able to buy, with the money paid them in lieu of rations, an abundance of fresh meats and vegetables; and most
of the companies managed at the same time to save a considerable fund for future use out of the surplus, so great
was the disparity between the cost of the food they bought
and that which the government wished to furnish them.

The indirect effect of all this stupidity—for it can be
called by no softer name—was almost as bad as its direct
results. The people at home, finding that the men in the field
were suffering for food, undertook to assist in supplying
them. With characteristic profusion they packed boxes and
sent them to their soldier friends and acquaintances, particularly during the first year of the war. Sometimes these
supplies were permitted to reach their destination, and
sometimes they were allowed to decay in a depot because of

some failure on the part of the sender to comply with the mysterious canons of official etiquette. In either case they were wasted. If they got to the army they were used wastefully by the men, who could not carry them and had no place of storage for them. If they were detained anywhere, they remained there until some change of front made it necessary to destroy them. There seemed to be nobody invested with sufficient authority to turn them to practical account. I remember a box of my own, packed with cooked meats, vegetables, fruits—all perishable—which got within three miles of my tent, but could get no farther, although I hired a farmer's wagon with which to bring it to camp, where my company was at that moment in sore need of its contents. There was some informality—the officer having it in charge could not tell me what—about the box itself, or its transmission, or its arrival, or something else, and so it could not be delivered to me, though I had the warrant of my colonel in writing, for receiving it. Dismissing my wagoner, I told the officer in charge that the contents of the box were of a perishable character, and that rather than have them wasted, I should be glad to have him accept the whole as a present to his mess; but he declined, on the ground that to accept the present would be a gross irregularity so long as there was an embargo upon the package. I received the box three months later, after its contents had become entirely worthless. Now this is but one of a hundred cases within my own knowledge, and it will serve to show the reader how the inefficiency of the subsistence department led to a wasteful expenditure of those private stores of food which constituted our only reserve for the future.

And there was never any improvement. From the beginning to the end of the war the commissariat was just sufficiently well managed to keep the troops in a state of semi-starvation. On one occasion the company of artillery to which I was attached lived for thirteen days, *in winter quarters,* on a daily dole of half a pound of corn meal per man, while food in abundance was stored within five miles of its camp—a railroad connecting the two points, and the wagons of the battery lying idle all the while. This happened because the subsistence department had not been officially informed of our transfer from one battalion to another, though the fact of the transfer was under their eyes, and the order of the chief of artillery making it was offered them in evidence. These officers were not to blame. They knew the temper of their chief, and had been taught the omnipotence of routine.

But it was in Richmond that routine was carried to its absurdest extremities. There, everything was done by rule except those things to which system of some sort would have been of advantage, and they were left at loose ends. Among other things a provost system was devised and brought to perfection during the time of martial law. Having once tasted the sweets of despotic rule, its chief refused to resign any part of his absolute sovereignty over the city, even when the reign of martial law ceased by limitation of time. His system of guards and passports was a very marvel of annoying inefficiency. It effectually blocked the way of every man who was intent upon doing his duty, while it gave unconscious but sure protection to spies, blockade-runners, deserters, and absentees without leave from the armies. It was omnipotent for the annoyance of soldier and citizen, but utterly worthless for any good purpose. If a soldier on furlough or even on detached duty arrived in Richmond, he was taken in charge by the provost guards at the railway station, marched to the soldiers' home or some other vile prison house, and kept there in durance during the whole time of his stay. It mattered not how legitimate his papers were, or how evident his correctness of purpose. The system required that he should be locked up, and locked up he was, in every case, until one plucky fellow made fight by appeal to the courts, and so compelled the abandonment of a practice for which there was never any warrant in law or necessity in fact.

Richmond being the railroad centre from which the various lines radiated, nearly every furloughed soldier and officer on leave was obliged to pass through the city, going home and returning. Now to any ordinary intelligence it would seem that a man bearing a full description of himself, and a furlough signed by his captain, colonel, brigadier, division-commander, lieutenant-general, and finally by Robert E. Lee as general-in-chief, might have been allowed to go peaceably to his home by the nearest route. But that was no ordinary intelligence which ruled Richmond. Its ability to find places in which to interfere was unlimited, and it decreed that no soldier should leave Richmond, either to go home or to return direct to the army, without a brown paper passport, signed by an officer appointed for that purpose, and countersigned by certain other persons whose authority to sign or countersign anything nobody was ever able to trace to its source. If any such precaution had been necessary, it would not have been so bad, or even being unnecessary, if there had been the slightest disposition on the part of these passport people to facilitate obedience to their own requirements, the long-suffering officers and men of the army would have uttered no word of complaint. But the facts were exactly the reverse. The passport officials rigidly maintained the integrity of their office hours, and neither entreaty nor persuasion would induce them in any case to anticipate by a single minute the hour for beginning, or to postpone the time of ending their daily duties. I stood one day in their office in a crowd of fellow soldiers and officers, some on furlough going home, some returning after a brief visit, and still others, like myself, going from one place to another under orders and on duty. The two trains by which most of us had to go were both to leave within an hour, and if we should lose them we must remain twenty-four hours longer in Richmond, where the hotel rate was then sixty dollars a day. In full view of these facts, the passport men, daintily dressed, sat there behind their railing, chatting and laughing for a full hour, suffering both trains to depart and all these men to be left over rather than do thirty minutes' work in advance of the improperly fixed office hour. It resulted from this system that many men on three or five days' leave lost nearly the whole of it in delays, going and returning. Many others were kept in Richmond for want of a passport until their furloughs expired, when they were arrested for absence without leave, kept three or four days in the guard-house, and then taken as prisoners to their commands, to which they had tried hard to go of their own motion at the proper time. Finally the abuse became so outrageous that General Lee, in his capacity of general-in-chief, issued a peremptory order forbidding anybody to interfere in any way with officers or soldiers traveling under his written authority.

But the complications of the passport system, before the issuing of that order, were endless. I went once with a friend in search of passports. As I had passed through Richmond a few weeks before, I fancied I knew all about the business of getting the necessary papers. Armed with our furloughs we went straight from the train to the passport office, and presenting our papers to the young man in charge, we asked for the brown paper permits which we must show upon leaving town. The young man prepared them and gave them to us, but this was no longer the end of the matter. These passports must be countersigned, and, strangely enough, my friend's required the sign-manual of Lieutenant X., whose office was in the lower part of the city, while mine must be signed by Lieutenant Y., who made his head-quarters some distance farther up town. As my friend and I were of precisely the same rank, came from the same command, were going to the same place, and held furloughs in exactly the same words, I shall not be deemed unreasonable when I declare my conviction that no imbecility, less fully developed than that which then governed Richmond, could possibly have discovered any reason for requiring that our passports should be countersigned by different people.

But with all the trouble it gave to men intent upon doing their duty, this cumbrous passport system was well-nigh worthless for any of the purposes whose accomplishment might have excused its existence. Indeed, in some cases it served to assist the very people it was intended to arrest. In one instance within my own knowledge, a soldier who wished to visit his home, some hundreds of miles away, failing to get a furlough, shouldered his musket and set out with no scrip for his journey, depending upon his familiarity with the passport system for the accomplishment of his purpose. Going to a railroad station, he planted himself at one of the entrances as a sentinel, and proceeded to demand passports of every comer. Then he got upon the train, and between stations he passed through the cars, again inspecting people's traveling papers. Nobody was surprised at the performance. It was not at all an unusual thing for a sentinel to go out with a train in this way, and nobody doubted that the man had been sent upon this errand.

On another occasion two officers of my acquaintance were going from a southern post to Virginia on some temporary duty, and in their orders there was a clause directing them to ''arrest and lodge in the nearest guard-house or jail'' all soldiers they might encounter who were absent without leave from their commands. As the train upon which they traveled approached Weldon, N. C., a trio of guards passed through the cars, inspecting passports. This was the third inspection inflicted upon the passengers within a few hours, and, weary of it, one of the two officers met the demand for his passport with a counter demand for the guards' authority to examine it. The poor fellows were there honestly enough, doubtless, doing a duty which was certainly not altogether pleasant, but they had been sent out on their mission with no attendant officer, and no scrap of paper to attest their authority, or even to avouch their right to be on the train at all; wherefore the journeying officer, exhibiting his own orders, proceeded to arrest them. Upon their arrival at Weldon, where their quarters were, he released them, but not without a lesson which provost guards in that vicinity remembered. I tell the story for the sake of showing how great a degree of laxity and carelessness prevailed in the department which was organized especially to enforce discipline by putting everybody under surveillance.

But this was not all. In Richmond, where the passport system had its birth, and where its annoying requirements were most sternly enforced against people having a manifest right to travel, there were still greater abuses. Will the reader believe that while soldiers, provided with the very best possible evidence of their right to enter and leave Richmond, were badgered and delayed as I have explained, in the passport office, the bits of brown paper over which so great an ado was made might be, and were, bought and sold by dealers? That such was the case I have the very best evidence, namely, that of my own senses. If the system was worth anything at all, if it was designed to accomplish any worthy end, its function was to prevent the escape of spies, blockade-runners, and deserters; and yet these were precisely the people who were least annoyed by it. By a system of logic peculiar to themselves, the provost marshal's people seem to have arrived at the conclusion that men deserting the army, acting as spies, or "running the blockade" to the North, were to be found only in Confederate uniforms, and against men wearing these the efforts of the department were especially directed. Non-military men had little difficulty in getting passports at will, and failing this there were brokers' shops in which they could buy them at a comparatively small cost. I knew one case in which an army officer in full uniform, hurrying through Richmond before the expiration of his leave, in order that he might be with his command in a battle then impending, was ordered about from one official to another in a vain search for the necessary passport, until he became discouraged and impatient. He finally went in despair to a Jew, and bought an illicit permit to go to his post of duty.

But even as against soldiers, except those who were manifestly entitled to visit Richmond, the system was by no means effective. More than one deserter, to my own knowledge, passed through Richmond in full uniform, though by what means they avoided arrest, when there were guards and passport inspectors at nearly every corner, I cannot guess.

At one time, when General Stuart, with his cavalry, was encamped within a few miles of the city, he discovered that his men were visiting Richmond by dozens, without leave, which, for some reason or other known only to the provost marshal's office, they were able to do without molestation. General Stuart, finding that this was the case, resolved to take the matter into his own hands, and accordingly with a troop of cavalry he made a descent upon the theatre one night, and arrested those of his men whom he found there. The provost marshal, who it would seem was more deeply concerned for the preservation of his own dignity than for the maintenance of discipline, sent a message to the great cavalier, threatening him with arrest if he should again presume to enter Richmond for the purpose of making arrests. Nothing could have pleased Stuart better. He replied that he should visit Richmond again the next night, with thirty horsemen; that he should patrol the streets in search of absentees from his command; and that General Winder might arrest him if he could. The jingling of spurs was loud in the streets that night, but the provost marshal made no attempt to arrest the defiant horseman.

Throughout the management of affairs in Richmond a cumbrous inefficiency was everywhere manifest. From the president, who insulted his premier for presuming to offer some advice about the conduct of the war, and quarreled with his generals because they failed to see the wisdom of a military movement suggested by himself, down to the pettiest clerk in a bureau, there was everywhere a morbid sensitiveness on the subject of personal dignity, and an exaggerated regard for routine, which seriously impaired the efficiency of the government and greatly annoyed the army. Under all the circumstances the reader will not be surprised to learn that the government at Richmond was by no means idolized by the men in the field.

The wretchedness of its management began to bear fruit early in the war, and the fruit was bitter in the mouths of the soldiers. Mr. Davis's evident hostility to Generals Beauregard and Johnston, which showed itself in his persistent refusal to let them concentrate their men, in his obstinate thwarting of all their plans, and in his interference with the details of army organization on which they were agreed—a hostility born, as General Thomas Jordan gives us to understand, of their failure to see the wisdom of his plan of campaign after Bull Run, which was to take the army across the lower Potomac at a point where it could never hope to recross, for the purpose of capturing a small force lying there under General Sickles—was not easily concealed; and the army was too intelligent not to know that a meddlesome and dictatorial president, on bad terms with his generals in the field, and bent upon thwarting their plans, was a very heavy load to carry. The generals held their peace, as a matter of course, but the principal facts were well known to officers and men, and when the time came, in the fall of 1861, for the election of a president under the permanent constitution (Mr. Davis having held office provisionally only, up to that time), there was a very decided disposition on the part of the troops to vote against him. They were told, however, that as there was no candidate opposed to him, he must be elected at any rate, and that the moral effect of showing a divided front to the enemy would be very bad indeed; and in this way only was the undivided vote of the army secured for him. The troops voted for Mr. Davis thus under stress of circumstances, in the hope that all would yet be well; but his subsequent course was not calculated to reinstate him in their confidence, and the wish that General Lee might see fit to usurp all the powers of government was a commonly expressed one, both in the army and in private life, during the last two years of the war.

The favoritism which governed nearly every one of the president's appointments was the leading, though not the only, ground of complaint. And truly the army had reason to murmur, when one of the president's pets was promoted all the way from lieutenant-colonel to lieutenant-general, having been but once in battle—and then only constructively so—on his way up, while colonels by the hundred, and brigadier and major generals by the score, who had been fighting hard and successfully all the time, were left as they were. And when this suddenly created general, almost without a show of resistance, surrendered one of the most important strongholds in the country, together with a veteran army of considerable size, is it any wonder that we questioned the wisdom of the president whose blind favoritism had dealt the cause so severe a blow? But not content with this, as soon as the surrendered general was exchanged the president tried to place him in command of the defenses of Richmond, then hard pressed by General Grant, and was only prevented from doing so by the man's own discovery that the troops would not willingly serve under him.

The extent to which presidential partiality and presidential intermeddling with affairs in the field were carried may be guessed, perhaps, from the fact that the Richmond *Examiner,* the newspaper which most truly reflected the sentiment of the people, found consolation for the loss of Vicksburg and New Orleans in the thought that the consequent cutting of the Confederacy in two freed the trans-Mississippi armies from paralyzing dictation. In its leading article for October 5, 1864, the *Examiner* said—

"The fall of New Orleans and the surrender of Vicksburg proved blessings to the cause beyond the Mississippi. It terminated the *régime* of pet generals. It put a stop to official piddling in the conduct of the armies and the plan of campaigns. The moment when it became impossible to send orders by telegraph to court officers, at the head of troops who despised them, was the moment of the turning tide."

So marked was the popular discontent, not with Mr. Davis only, but with the entire government and Congress as well, that a Richmond newspaper at one time dared to suggest a counter revolution as the only means left of saving the cause from the strangling it was receiving at the hands of its guardians in Richmond. And the suggestion seemed so very reasonable and timely that it startled nobody, except perhaps a congressman or two who had no stomach for field service.

The approach of the end wrought no change in the temper of the government, and one of its last acts puts in the strongest light its disposition to sacrifice the interests of the army to the convenience of the court. When the evacuation of Richmond was begun, a train load of provisions was sent by General Lee's order from one of the interior *dépôts* to Amelia Court House, for the use of the retreating army, which was without food and must march to that point before it could receive a supply. But the president and his followers were in haste to leave the capital, and needed the train, wherefore it was not allowed to remain at Amelia Court House long enough to be unloaded, but was hurried on to Richmond, where its cargo was thrown out to facilitate the flight of the president and his personal followers, while the starving army was left to suffer in an utterly exhausted country, with no source of supply anywhere within its reach. The surrender of the army was already inevitable, it is true, but that fact in no way justified this last, crowning act of selfishness and cruelty.

CHAPTER 10

THE END, AND AFTER

———————— ◆ ————————

IT IS impossible to say precisely when the conviction became general in the South that we were to be beaten. I cannot even decide at what time I myself began to think the cause a hopeless one, and I have never yet found one of my fellow-Confederates, though I have questioned many of them, who could tell me with any degree of certainty the history of his change from confidence to despondency. We schooled ourselves from the first to think that we should ultimately win, and the habit of thinking so was too strong to be easily broken by adverse happenings. Having undertaken to make good our declaration of independence, we refused to admit, even to ourselves, the possibility of failure. It was a part of our soldierly and patriotic duty to believe that ultimate success was to be ours, and Stuart only uttered the common thought of army and people, when he said, "We are bound to believe that, anyhow." We were convinced, beyond the possibility of a doubt, of the absolute righteousness of our cause, and in spite of history we persuaded ourselves that a people battling for the right could not fail in the end. And so our hearts went on hoping for success long after our heads had learned to expect failure.

Besides all this, we never gave verbal expression to the doubts we felt, or even to the longing, which must have been universal, for the end. It was our religion to believe in the triumph of our cause, and it was heresy of the rankest sort to doubt it or even to admit the possibility of failure. It was ours to fight on indefinitely, and to the future belonged the award of victory to our arms. We did not allow ourselves even the poor privilege of wishing that the struggle might end, except as we coupled the wish with a pronounced confidence in our ability to make the end what we desired it to be. I remember very well the stern rebuke administered by an officer to as gallant a fellow as any in the army, who, in utter weariness and wretchedness, in the trenches at Spotsylvania Court House, after a night of watching in a drenching rain, said that he hoped the campaign then opening might be the last one of the war. His plea that he also hoped the war would end as we desired availed him nothing. To be weary in the cause was offense enough, and the officer gave warning that another such expression would subject the culprit to trial by court-martial. In this he only spoke the common mind. We had enlisted for the war, and a thought of weariness was hardly better than a wish for surrender. This was the temper in which we began the campaign of 1864, and so far as I have been able to discover, it underwent little change afterwards. Even during the final retreat, though there were many desertions soon after Richmond was left behind, not one of us who remained despaired of the end we sought. We discussed the comparative strategic merits of the line we had left and the new one we hoped to make on the Roanoke River, and we wondered where the seat of government would be, but not one word was said about a probable or possible surrender. Nor was the army alone in this. The people who were being left behind were confident that they should see us again shortly, on our way to Richmond's recapture.

Up to the hour of the evacuation of Richmond, the newspapers were as confident as ever of victory. During the fall of 1864 they even believed, or professed to believe, that our triumph was already at hand. The Richmond *Whig* of October 5, 1864, said: ''That the present condition of affairs, compared with that of any previous year at the same season, at least since 1861, is greatly in our favor, we think can hardly be denied.'' In the same article it said: ''That General Lee can keep Grant out of Richmond from this time until doomsday, if he should be tempted to keep up the trial so long, we are as confident as we can be of anything whatever.'' The *Examiner* of September 24, 1864, said in its leading editorial: ''The final struggle for the possession of Richmond and of Virginia is now near. This war draws to a close. If Richmond is held by the South till the first of November it will be ours forever more; for the North will never throw another huge army into the abyss where so many lie; and the war will conclude, beyond a doubt, with the independence of the Southern States.'' In its issue for October 7, 1864, the same paper began its principal editorial article with this paragraph: ''One month of spirit and energy now, and the campaign is over, and the war is over. We do not mean that if the year's campaign end favorably for us, McClellan will be elected as Yankee President. That may come, or may not come; but no part of our chance for an honorable peace and independence rests upon that. Let who will be Yankee President, with the failure of Grant and Sherman this year, the war ends. And with Sherman's army already isolated and cut off in Georgia, and Grant unable either to take or besiege Richmond, we have only to make one month's exertion in improving our advantages, and then it may safely be said that the fourth year's campaign, and with it the war itself, is one gigantic failure." The Richmond *Whig* of September 8, 1864, with great gravity copied from the Wytheville *Dispatch* an article beginning as follows: "Believing as we do that the war of subjugation is virtually over, we deem it not improper to make a few suggestions relative to the treatment of Yankees after the war is over. Our soldiers know how to treat them now, but *then* a different treatment will be necessary." And so they talked all the time.

Much of this was mere whistling to keep our courage up, of course, but we tried very hard to believe all these pleasant things, and in a measure we succeeded. And yet I think we must have known from the beginning of the campaign of 1864 that the end was approaching, and that it could not be other than a disastrous one. We knew very well that General Lee's army was smaller than it ever had been before. We knew, too, that there were no reinforcements to be had from any source. The conscription had put every man worth counting into the field already, and the little army that met General Grant in the Wilderness represented all that remained of the Confederate strength in Virginia. In the South matters were at their worst, and we knew that not a man could come thence to our assistance. Lee mustered a total strength of about sixty-six thousand men, when we marched out of winter quarters and began in the Wilderness that long struggle which ended nearly a year later at Appomattox. With that army alone the war was to be fought out, and we had to shut our eyes to facts very resolutely, that we might not see how certainly we were to be crushed. And we did shut our eyes so successfully as to hope in a vague, irrational way, for the impossible, to the very end. In the Wilderness we held our own against every assault, and the visible punishment we inflicted upon the foe was so great that hardly any man in our army expected to see a Federal force on our side of the river at daybreak next morning. We thought that General Grant was as badly hurt as Hooker had been on the same field, and confidently expected him to retreat during the night. When he moved by his left flank to Spotsylvania instead, we understood what manner of man he was, and knew that the persistent pounding, which of all things we were least able to endure, had begun. When at last we settled down in the trenches around Petersburg, we ought to have known that the end was rapidly drawing near. We congratulated ourselves instead upon the fact that we had inflicted a heavier loss than we had suffered, and buckled on our armor anew.

If General Grant had failed to break our power of resistance by his sledge-hammer blows, it speedily became evident that he would be more successful in wearing it away by the constant friction of a siege. Without fighting a battle he was literally destroying our army. The sharp-shooting was incessant, and the bombardment hardly less so, and under it all our numbers visibly decreased day by day. During the first two months of the siege my own company, which numbered about a hundred and fifty men, lost sixty, in killed and wounded, an average of a man a day, and while our list of casualties was greater than that of many other commands, there were undoubtedly some companies and regiments which suffered more than we. The reader will readily understand that an army already weakened by years of war, with no source from which to recruit its ranks, could not stand this daily waste for any great length of time. We were in a state of atrophy for which there was no remedy except that of freeing the Negroes and making soldiers of them, which Congress was altogether too loftily sentimental to think of for a moment.

There was no longer any room for hope except in a

superstitious belief that Providence would in some way interfere in our behalf, and to that very many betook themselves for comfort. This shifting upon a supernatural power the task we had failed to accomplish by human means rapidly bred many less worthy superstitions among the troops. The general despondency, which amounted almost to despair, doubtless helped to bring about this result, and the great religious "revival" contributed to it in no small degree. I think hardly any man in that army entertained a thought of coming out of the struggle alive. The only question with each was when his time was to come, and a sort of gloomy fatalism took possession of many minds. Believing that they must be killed sooner or later, and that the hour and the manner of their deaths were unalterably fixed, many became singularly reckless, and exposed themselves with the utmost carelessness to all sorts of unnecessary dangers.

"I'm going to be killed pretty soon," said as brave a man as I ever knew, to me one evening. "I never flinched from a bullet until to-day, and now I dodge every time one whistles within twenty feet of me."

I tried to persuade him out of the belief, and even got for him a dose of valerian with which to quiet his nerves. He took the medicine, but assured me that he was not nervous in the least.

"My time is coming, that's all," he said; "and I don't care. A few days more or less don't signify much." An hour later the poor fellow's head was blown from his shoulders as he stood by my side.

One such incident—and there were many of them— served to confirm a superstitious belief in presentiments which a hundred failures of fulfillment were unable to shake. Meantime the revival went on. Prayer-meetings were held in every tent. Testaments were in every hand, and a sort of religious ecstasy took possession of the army. The men had ceased to rely upon the skill of their leaders or the strength of our army for success, and not a few of them hoped now for a miraculous interposition of supernatural power in our behalf. Men in this mood make the best of soldiers, and at no time were the fighting qualities of the Southern army better than during the siege. Under such circumstances men do not regard death, and even the failure of any effort they were called upon to make wrought no demoralization among troops who had persuaded themselves that the Almighty held victory in store for them, and would give it them in due time. What cared they for the failure of mere human efforts, when they were persuaded that through such failures God was leading us to ultimate victory? Disaster seemed only to strengthen the faith of many. They saw in it a needed lesson in humility, and an additional reason for believing that God meant to bring about victory by his own and not by human strength. They did their soldierly duties perfectly. They held danger and fatigue alike in contempt. It was their duty as Christian men to obey orders without question, and they did so in the thought that to do otherwise was to sin.

That the confidence bred of these things should be of a gloomy kind was natural enough, and the gloom was not dispelled, certainly, by the conviction of every man that he was assisting at his own funeral. Failure, too, which was worse than death, was plainly inevitable in spite of it all. We persisted, as I have said, in vaguely hoping and trying to believe that success was still to be ours, and to that end we shut our eyes to the plainest facts, refusing to admit the truth which was everywhere evident, namely, that our efforts had failed, and that our cause was already in its death struggles. But we must have known all this, nevertheless, and our diligent cultivation of an unreasonable hopefulness served in no sensible degree to raise our spirits.

Even positive knowledge does not always bring belief. I doubt if a condemned man, who finds himself in full bodily health, ever quite believes that he is to die within the hour, however certainly he may know the fact; and our condition was not unlike that of condemned men.

When at last the beginning of the end came, in the evacuation of Richmond and the effort to retreat, everything seemed to go to pieces at once. The best disciplinarians in the army relaxed their reins. The best troops became disorganized, and hardly any command marched in a body. Companies were mixed together, parts of each being separated by detachments of others. Flying citizens in vehicles of every conceivable sort accompanied and embarrassed the columns. Many commands marched heedlessly on without orders, and seemingly without a thought of whither they were going. Others mistook the meaning of their orders, and still others had instructions which it was impossible to obey in any case. At Amelia Court House we should have found a supply of provisions. General Lee had ordered a train load to meet him there, but, as I have stated in a previous chapter, the interests of the starving army had been sacrificed to the convenience or the cowardice of the president and his personal following. The train had been hurried on to Richmond and its precious cargo of food thrown out there, in order that Mr. Davis and his people might retreat rapidly and comfortably from the abandoned capital. Then began the desertion of which we have heard so much. Up to that time, as far as I can learn, if desertions had occurred at all they had not become general; but now that the government, in flying from the foe, had cut off our only supply of provisions, what were the men to do? Many of them wandered off in search of food,

with no thought of deserting at all. Many others followed
the example of the government, and fled; but a singularly
large proportion of the little whole stayed and starved to
the last. And it was no technical or metaphorical starvation
which we had to endure, either, as a brief statement of my
own experience will show. The battery to which I was
attached was captured near Amelia Court House, and
within a mile or two of my home. Seven men only escaped,
and as I knew intimately everybody in the neighborhood, I
had no trouble in getting horses for these to ride. Applying
to General Lee in person for instructions, I was ordered
to march on, using my own judgment, and rendering what
service I could in the event of a battle. In this independent
fashion I marched with much better chances than most
of the men had, to get food, and yet during three days and
nights our total supply consisted of one ear of corn to the
man, and we divided that with our horses.

The end came, technically, at Appomattox, but of the real
difficulties of the war the end was not yet. The trials and
the perils of utter disorganization were still to be endured,
and as the condition in which many parts of the South
were left by the fall of the Confederate government was an
anomalous one, some account of it seems necessary to the
completeness of this narrative.

Our principal danger was from the lawless bands of
marauders who infested the country, and our greatest difficulty in dealing with them lay in the utter absence of constituted authority of any sort. Our country was full of
highwaymen—not the picturesque highwaymen of whom
fiction and questionable history tell us, those gallant, generous fellows whose purse-cutting proclivities seem mere
peccadilloes in the midst of so many virtues; not these, by
any means, but plain highwaymen of the most brutal description possible, and destitute even of the merit of pre-

senting a respectable appearance. They were simply the offscourings of the two armies and of the suddenly freed Negro population—deserters from fighting regiments on both sides, and Negro desperadoes, who found common ground upon which to fraternize in their common depravity. They moved about in bands, from two to ten strong, cutting horses out of plows, plundering helpless people, and wantonly destroying valuables which they could not carry away. At the house of one of my friends where only ladies lived, a body of these men demanded dinner, which was given them. They then required the mistress of the mansion to fill their canteens with sorghum molasses, which they immediately proceeded to pour over the carpets and furniture of the parlor. Outrages were of every-day enactment, and there was no remedy. There was no State, county, or municipal government in existence among us. We had no courts, no justices of the peace, no sheriffs, no officers of any kind invested with a shadow of authority, and there were not men enough in the community, at first, to resist the marauders, comparatively few of the surrendered soldiers having found their way home as yet. Those districts in which the Federal armies were stationed were peculiarly fortunate. The troops gave protection to the people, and the commandants of posts constituted a government able to enforce order, to which outraged or threatened people could appeal. But these favored sections were only a small part of the whole. The troops were not distributed in detached bodies over the country, but were kept in considerable masses at strategic points, lest a guerrilla war should succeed regular hostilities; and so the greater part of the country was left wholly without law, at a time when law was most imperatively needed. I mention this, not to the discredit of the victorious army or of its officers. They could not wisely have done otherwise. If the disbanded

Confederates had seen fit to inaugurate a partisan warfare, as many of the Federal commanders believed they would, they could have annoyed the army of occupation no little; and so long as the temper of the country in this matter was unknown, it would have been in the last degree improper to station small bodies of troops in exposed situations. Common military prudence dictated the massing of the troops, and as soon as it became evident that we had no disposition to resist further, but were disposed rather to render such assistance as we could in restoring and maintaining order, everything was done which could be done to protect us. It is with a good deal of pleasure that I bear witness to the uniform disposition shown by such Federal officers as I came in contact with at this time, to protect all quiet citizens, to restore order, and to forward the interests of the community they were called upon to govern. In one case I went with a fellow-Confederate to the headquarters nearest me—eighteen miles away,—and reported the doings of some marauders in my neighborhood, which had been especially outrageous. The general in command at once made a detail of cavalry and instructed its chief to go in pursuit of the highwaymen, and to bring them to him, dead or alive. They were captured, marched at a double-quick to the camp, and shot forthwith, by sentence of a drum-head court-martial, a proceeding which did more than almost anything else could have done, to intimidate other bands of a like kind. At another time I took to the same officer's camp a number of stolen horses which a party of us had managed to recapture from a sleeping band of desperadoes. Some of the horses we recognized as the property of our neighbors, some we did not know at all, and one or two were branded "C. S." and "U. S." The general promptly returned all the identified horses, and lent all the others to farmers in need of them.

After a little time most of the ex-soldiers returned to their homes, and finding that there were enough of us in the county in which I lived to exercise a much-needed police supervision if we had the necessary authority, we sent a committee of citizens to Richmond to report the facts to the general in command of the district. He received our committee very cordially, expressed great pleasure in the discovery that citizens were anxious to maintain order until a reign of law could be restored, and granted us leave to organize ourselves into a military police, with officers acting under written authority from him; to patrol the country; to disarm all improper or suspicious persons; to arrest and turn over to the nearest provost marshal all wrong-doers, and generally to preserve order by armed surveillance. To this he attached but one condition, namely, that we should hold ourselves bound in honor to assist any United States officer who might require such service of us, in the suppression of guerrilla warfare. To this we were glad enough to assent, as the thing we dreaded most at that time was the inauguration of a hopeless, irregular struggle, which would destroy the small chance left us of rebuilding our fortunes and restoring our wasted country to prosperity. We governed the county in which we lived, until the establishment of a military post at the county seat relieved us of the task, and the permission given us thus to stamp out lawlessness saved our people from the alternative of starvation or dependence upon the bounty of the government. It was seed-time, and without a vigorous maintenance of order our fields could not have been planted at all.

It is difficult to comprehend, and impossible to describe, the state of uncertainty in which we lived at this time. We had surrendered at discretion, and had no way of discovering or even of guessing what terms were to be given us. We were cut off almost wholly from trustworthy news, and in the absence of papers were unable even to rest conjecture upon the expression of sentiment at the North. Rumors we had in plenty, but so many of them were clearly false that we were forced to reject them all as probably untrue. When we heard it confidently asserted that General Alexander had made a journey to Brazil and brought back a tempting offer to emigrants, knowing all the time that if he had gone he must have made the trip within the extraordinarily brief period of a few weeks, it was difficult to believe other news which reached us through like channels, though much of it ultimately proved true. I think nobody in my neighborhood believed the rumor of Mr. Lincoln's assassination until it was confirmed by a Federal soldier whom I questioned upon the subject one day, a week or two after the event. When we knew that the rumor was true, we deemed it the worst news we had heard since the surrender. We distrusted President Johnson more than any one else. Regarding him as a renegade Southerner, we thought it probable that he would endeavor to prove his loyalty to the Union by extra severity to the South, and we confidently believed he would revoke the terms offered us in Mr. Lincoln's amnesty proclamation; wherefore there was a general haste to take the oath and so to secure the benefit of the dead president's clemency before his successor should establish harsher conditions. We should have regarded Mr. Lincoln's death as a calamity, even if it had come about by natural means, and coming as it did through a crime committed in our name, it seemed doubly a disaster.

With the history of the South during the period of reconstruction, all readers are familiar, and it is only the state of affairs between the time of the surrender and the beginning of the rebuilding, that I have tried to describe in this chapter. But the picture would be inexcusably in-

complete without some mention of the Negroes. Their behavior both during and after the war may well surprise
anybody not acquainted with the character of the race.
When the men of the South were nearly all in the army,
the Negroes were left in large bodies on the plantations
with nobody to control them except the women and a few
old or infirm men. They might have been insolent, insubordi-
nate, and idle, if they had chosen. They might have gained
their freedom by asserting it. They might have overturned
the social and political fabric at any time, *and they knew
all this too.* They were intelligent enough to know that
there was no power on the plantations capable of resisting
any movement they might choose to make. They did know,
too, that the success of the Federal arms would give them
freedom. The fact was talked about everywhere, and no
effort was made to keep the knowledge of it from them.
They knew that to assert their freedom was to give immediate success to the Union cause. Most of them coveted
freedom, too, as the heartiness with which they afterwards
accepted it abundantly proves. And yet they remained
quiet, faithful, and diligent throughout, very few of them
giving trouble of any sort, even on plantations where only
a few women remained to control them. The reason for all
this must be sought in the Negro character, and we of the
South, knowing that character thoroughly, trusted it im-
plicitly. We left our homes and our helpless ones in the
keeping of the Africans of our households, without any
hesitation whatever. We knew these faithful and affectionate people too well to fear that they would abuse such a
trust. We concealed nothing from them, and they knew
quite as well as we did the issues at stake in the war.

The Negro is constitutionally loyal to his obligations as
he understands them, and his attachments, both local and
personal, are uncommonly strong. He speedily forgets an

injury, but never a kindness, and so he was not likely to
rise in arms against the helpless women and children whom
he had known intimately and loved almost reverentially
from childhood, however strongly he desired the freedom
which such a rising would secure to him. It was a failure
to appreciate these peculiarities of the Negro character
which led John Brown into the mistake that cost him his
life. Nothing is plainer than that he miscalculated the
difficulty of exciting the colored people to insurrection. He
went to Harper's Ferry, confident that when he should declare his purposes, the Negroes would flock to his standard
and speedily crown his effort with success. They remained
quietly at work instead, many of them hoping, doubtless,
that freedom for themselves and their fellows might somehow be wrought out, but they were wholly unwilling to
make the necessary war upon the whites to whom they were
attached by the strongest possible bonds of affection. And
so throughout the war they acted after their kind, waiting
for the issue with the great, calm patience which is their
most universal characteristic.

When the war ended, leaving everything in confusion,
the poor blacks hardly knew what to do, but upon the
whole they acted with great modesty, much consideration
for their masters, and singular wisdom. A few depraved
ones took to bad courses at once, but their number was re-
markably small. Some others, with visionary notions, betook themselves to the cities in search of easier and more
profitable work than any they had ever done, and many of
these suffered severely from want before they found employment again. The great majority waited patiently for
things to adjust themselves in their new conditions, going
on with their work meanwhile, and conducting themselves
with remarkable modesty. I saw much of them at this time,
and I heard of no case in which a Negro voluntarily re-

minded his master of the changed relations existing between them, or in any other way offended against the strictest rules of propriety.

At my own home the master of the mansion assembled his Negroes immediately after the surrender; told them they were free, and under no obligation whatever to work for him; and explained to them the difficulty he found in deciding what kind of terms he ought to offer them, inasmuch as he was wholly ignorant upon the subject of the wages of agricultural laborers. He told them, however, that if they wished to go on with the crop, he would give them provisions and clothing as before, and at the end of the year would pay them as high a rate of wages as any paid in the neighborhood. To this every Negro on the place agreed, all of them protesting that they wanted no better terms than for their master to give them at the end of the year whatever he thought they had earned. They lost not an hour from their work, and the life upon the plantation underwent no change whatever until its master was forced by a pressure of debt to sell his land. I give the history of the adjustment on this plantation as a fair example of the way in which ex-masters and ex-slaves were disposed to deal with each other.

There were cases in which no such harmonious adjustment could be effected, but, so far as my observation extended, these were exceptions to the common rule, and even now, after a lapse of nine years, a very large proportion of the Negroes remain, either as hired laborers or as renters of small farms, on the plantations on which they were born.